Collins · *do brilliantly !*

RevisionGuide

GCSE ICT

Published by HarperCollins*Publishers* Ltd
77-85 Fulham Palace Road
London W6 8JB

www.CollinsEducation.com
On-line support for schools and colleges

First published 2004
10 9 8 7 6 5 4 3 2 1

ISBN 0 00 720417 5

British Library Cataloguing in Publication Data
A catalogue record for this book is available from the British Library.

Edited by Catriona Watson-Brown
Series and book design by Sally Boothroyd
Cartoon illustrations by Sarah Wimperis
Index compiled by Julie Rimington
Production by Katie Butler
Printed and bound by Printing Express, Hong Kong

Photographs
The Authors and Publishers are grateful to the following for permission to reproduce
photographs:
Hewlett Packard: pp. 1, 2, 3, 6, 7, 8, 10,
Science Photo Library: page 11
All other photographs were taken on behalf of Collins Educational by Mike Watson.

Every effort has been made to contact the holders of copyright material, but if any
have been inadvertently overlooked, the Publishers will be pleased to make the
necessary arrangements at the first opportunity.

Collins · *do brilliantly !*

Revision**Guide**

GCSE ICT

- **Denise Walmsley, Peter Sykes and Henry Robson**

- **Series editor: Jayne de Courcy**

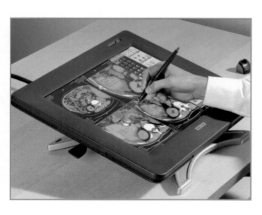

CONTENTS AND REVISION PLANNER

	On syllabus	Revise again	Revised & understood
SECTION I			
UNIT 1: INPUT DEVICES			
Revision session 1: Types of input devices 1			
2: Other ways of capturing data 4			
UNIT 2: OUTPUT DEVICES			
Revision session 1: Common output devices 6			
2: Other output devices 8			
UNIT 3: COMPUTER SYSTEMS HARDWARE			
Revision session 1: Inside the computer 9			
2: Different types of computer 10			
UNIT 4: STORAGE			
Revision session 1: Internal memory 12			
2: Backing storage 13			
UNIT 5: LINKING COMPUTERS TOGETHER			
Revision session 1: Computers communicating 15			
2: Networks 16			
UNIT 6: LEGAL ISSUES			
Revision session 1: Copyright and misuse 18			
2: Data Protection Act 19			
UNIT 7: SOCIAL ISSUES			
Revision session 1: Computers in everyday life 21			
2: Computers at work 22			
UNIT 8: HEALTH AND SAFETY			
Revision session 1: Computers, health and safety 23			
2: Keeping data safe 24			
UNIT 9: DIFFERENT TYPES OF PROCESSING			
Revision session 1: Batch processing 26			
2: Online/Real-time processing 28			
UNIT 10: SYSTEMS CYCLE			
Revision session 1: Steps of the system cycle 29			
2: Systems analysis 30			
3: Systems design, development, testing and implementation 31			
UNIT 11: SYSTEMS SOFTWARE			
Revision session 1: Operating systems and user-interface software 33			
2: Translators and utilities 34			
UNIT 12: BUSINESS APPLICATIONS SOFTWARE			
Revision session 1: Word processors and desktop publishers 35			
2: Spreadsheets 37			
3: Databases 38			
4: Computer-aided design (CAD) 40			
5: The Internet and e-mail 41			
UNIT 13: DATA LOGGING AND CONTROL			
Revision session 1: Data logging 43			
2: Control systems 44			
UNIT 14: APPLICATIONS			
Revision session 1: Multimedia systems 45			
2: Applications in the home 46			
3: Business applications 47			
4: Expert systems 50			
UNIT 15: EXAM PRACTICE			
Short course sample questions and answers 51			
Questions to try 53			
Full course sample questions and answers 54			
Questions to try 56			

SECTION 2 OCR COURSEWORK 57
UNIT 1: PROJECT 1A 58
UNIT 2: PROJECT 1B 67
UNIT 3: PROJECT 2 73
Session   1: Analysis 73
       2: Designing the data structure 77
       3: Designing the interface 81
       4: Designing the outputs 85
       5: Hardware and software requirements 88
       6: Implementing/developing the data structure
          and inputs and outputs 90
       7: Evidence of software features and
          other software combined 95
       8: Testing 98
       9: User documentation 101
       10: Evaluation 104

SECTION 3 AQA COURSEWORK: SET ASSIGNMENT 107
Task   1: Analysis 107
       2: Analysis 111
       1: Design 114
       1: Implementation 117
       1: Evaluation 119
       2: Design 121
       2: Implementation 125
       2: Testing 127
       2: Evaluation 129

SECTION 4 AQA COURSEWORK: PROJECT 131
UNIT 1: ANALYSIS 131
Session   1: Overview: How to begin research 131
       2: Introducing your analysis 133
       3: Identifying and analysing sub-problems 134
       4: Different ways of tackling the sub-problems 135
       5: Determining the outcome 137
       6: Describing the relationships between
          the sub-problems 139
       7: Specifying desired outcomes and
          performance criteria 140
UNIT 2: DESIGN
Session   1: Designing for publishing sub-problems 142
       2: Designing for a database sub-problem 147
       3: Designing for a spreadsheet sub-problem 154
UNIT 3: IMPLEMENTATION
Session   1: Implementing publishing sub-problems 157
       2: Implementing database sub-problems 161
       3: Implementing spreadsheet sub-problems 166
UNIT 4: TESTING
Session   1: Testing database sub-problems 168
       2: Testing a spreadsheet sub-problem 172
UNIT 5: EVALUATION
Session   1: Evaluating a publishing solution 173
       2: Evaluating a database solution 174
UNIT 6: USER GUIDE
Session   1: Producing a user guide 175
Check yourself answers and comments 178
Index 189

ABOUT THIS BOOK

Exams are about much more than just repeating memorised facts, so we have planned this book to make your revision as active and effective as possible.

How?

- by breaking down the content into manageable chunks (Sessions and Revision Sessions)

- by showing you exactly what coursework advisers are looking for (Coursework sections)

- by testing your understanding at every step of the way (Check Yourself Questions)

- by providing extra information to help you aim for the very top grade (A* Extras)

- by listing the most likely exam questions for each topic (Question Spotters)

- by giving you invaluable examiner's guidance about exam technique (Exam Practice)

Revision Sessions

- Section 1 covers the theory elements you need for your ICT exam papers. Whether you are sitting **Foundation** papers, **Higher** papers, **short course** or **full course**, what you need is here.

- Each topic that you need to revise for your exam is divided into a number of **short Revision sessions**. You should be able to read through each of these in no more than 20–25 minutes. That is the maximum amount of time that you should spend on revising without taking a short break.

- Ask your teacher for a copy of your own exam board's **GCSE ICT** specification. Tick off on the Contents list in this book each of the Revision sessions that you need to cover. It will probably be most of them if you are taking the full course.

Coursework sections

- Sections 2, 3 and 4 of the book contain lots of information on what examiners are looking for in order to award high marks for a coursework project or assignment. There's also plenty of help with **planning** and **presentation**. Section 2 relates specifically to **OCR** (see page 57 for an overview) and Sections 3 and 4 relate specifically to **AQA** (see pages 106 and 130 for overviews).

? CHECK YOURSELF QUESTIONS

- At the end of each Revision session in Section 1, there are some Check Yourself Questions. By trying these questions, you will immediately find out whether you have understood and remembered what you have read in the Revision session. **Answers** are at the back of the book, along with **extra hints and guidance**.

- If you manage to answer all the Check Yourself Questions for a session correctly, then you can confidently tick off this topic in the grid provided in the Contents list. If not, you will need to tick the 'Revise again' box to remind yourself to return to this topic later in your revision programme.

⚡ A* EXTRA

- These boxes contain some **extra information** which you need to learn if you are aiming to achieve the **very top grade**. If you have the chance to use these additional facts in your exam, it could make the difference between a good answer and a very good answer.

🔅 QUESTION SPOTTER

- It's obviously important to revise the facts, but it's also helpful to know how you might need to **use** this information in your exam.

- The authors, who have been involved with examining for many years, know the sorts of questions that are most likely to be asked on each topic. They have put together these Question Spotter boxes so that they can help you to **focus your revision**.

Exam Practice

- Unit 15 gives you help with **answering exam questions well**. There are students' answers to some questions, with examiner's comments highlighting how to achieve full marks.

- There are also **questions for you to try**, with answers given at the back of the book for you to check your own answers against.

About your GCSE ICT course

GCSE specifications

- All the ICT GCSE specifications are quite similar in content. The standard of work is the same because all the specifications have to meet a nationally agreed standard. This book is aimed mainly at the AQA and OCR specifications, and so has separate coursework sections for these boards. However, the theory Revision sessions in Section 1 cover the content found in **all** specifications for GCSE ICT.

Examinations and Coursework

- For the short-course GCSE examination, there is one exam paper; for the full course, you may sit an additional paper. Content that is only required if you are sitting the **full course** is clearly marked in this book as follows:

  FC full course (both AQA and OCR)

  FC(A) full course for AQA students

  FC(O) full course for OCR students

- Generally, you will need to do more than one piece of work for your coursework. This is because there is such a range of software packages, and you will need to show your expertise in a variety of ways.

- All ICT GCSE specifications put greater emphasis on assessed coursework than on the terminal exam. Coursework is worth 60% of the overall GCSE mark, whether you are doing a short-course or full-course GCSE. This means that if you get full marks for your coursework, you already have 60% of your final mark before you answer any exam questions!

What is assessed?

- In GCSE ICT, you have to develop your skills in using a variety of software packages, such as desktop publishers, databases, spreadsheets and word processors. You also have to learn all the related theory work, such as how to test systems, how to document systems and how to analyse and design systems.

- In addition, there are other theory aspects which are quite factual, and you need to learn these in isolation from your practical work. Examples of these topics are the laws governing ICT, Health and Safety, different examples of hardware and software, and applications they are used for.

Foundation and Higher tier papers

- If you decide to do the Foundation examination papers rather than the Higher tier examination papers, you will find the questions much easier, but the maximum grade you will be aiming for is a C grade.

- The Higher tier papers are aimed at D-grade candidates and above, right up to A*. The coursework projects or assignments are identical, but at Foundation level you will not be expected to aim for such high marks.

- When you have completed your coursework, your teacher will be able to advise you which is the most appropriate tier for you to enter.

Higher tier							
A*	A	B	C	D	E	F	G
				Foundation tier			

COURSEWORK 60%

GCSE ICT

EXAMINATION 40%

UNIT 1: INPUT DEVICES

Types of input devices

➪ Keyboard

- A **keyboard** is the commonest way to enter data into a computer.

- Keys represent **letters**, **numbers** and **special symbols**.

- Most keyboards are known as **QWERTY** keyboards because the first few keys on the top row of letters spell 'qwerty'.

> **⚡ A* EXTRA**
>
> Some special 'concept keyboards' have only a few keys for selecting limited options. Examples can be seen in restaurants and fast-food outlets.

1.1 *a keyboard*

➪ Mouse

- A **mouse** is a hand-held device with one, two or three **buttons**.

- Buttons are used to **select from menus**, **move objects around the screen**, and **paint or draw**.

- Under the mouse is a **ball**, which rolls and comes into contact with sensors. It allows the device to move across a flat surface.

- The user can control where the pointer on the screen (the **cursor**) is by moving the mouse around.

1.2 *a mouse*

➪ Tracker ball/Joystick

- A **tracker ball** looks like an upside-down mouse with a ball on top. The user rolls the ball to control the cursor. The device stays still.

- A **joystick** is similar to a tracker ball, except a stick replaces the ball.

- Tracker balls and joysticks are usually used for playing action computer games.

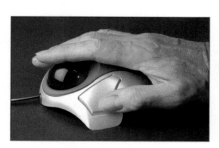

1.3 *a tracker ball and a joystick*

> **💡 QUESTION SPOTTER**
>
> ▸ You may be given pictures of a variety of devices and asked to name them.
> ▸ Alternatively, a list of devices could be provided, and you will need to circle two devices which are input devices.

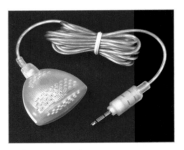

1.4 *a microphone*

▷ Microphone

- A **microphone** is for the **input of sound**, which may take various forms, e.g. voice, music, etc.

- In a voice recognition system, software is used to convert voice into text or to activate menu options.

▷ Midi instruments

- **Midi instruments** are **musical instruments** which send and receive electronic data.

1.5 *a midi keyboard*

- If the midi instruments are connected to the computer, the musical data can be stored as a file, displayed on screen and edited ready for playback.

1.6 *a digital camera*

▷ Digital camera

- In a **digital camera**, light received through the lens is converted to **digital signals** by sensors.

- The digital data captured about the image is stored and can be later used like any other image file.

▷ Video digitiser

- A **video digitiser** enables video signals from a standard video camera to be read into a computer and stored as a digital data for later use.

⇨ Scanner

- A **scanner** is like a photocopier. It scans the source material with a **laser beam**, but instead of printing copies, it transmits the image to the computer as digital code, which can be saved as a file.

1.7 *a scanner*

⇨ Graphics tablet

- A **graphics tablet** is a flat pad on which you can write or draw with a **pressure-sensitive stylus** (like a pen).

- It is used for **artwork**, **computer-aided design** (CAD) and cartography.

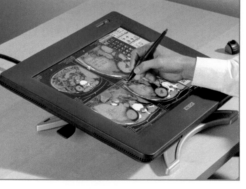

1.8 *a graphics tablet*

⇨ Sensor

- A **sensor** captures **physical measurements** for conversion to digital data which can be used by the computer.

- Sensors can be used to measure **heat**, **light**, **sound**, **pressure**, **humidity** and many other physical measurements.

? CHECK YOURSELF QUESTIONS

Q1 Name the two most common input devices.

Q2 Which input devices could be used to capture music?

Q3 Which input devices could be used to capture existing image data?

Answers are on page 178.

Other ways of capturing data

➪ Bar-code reader **FC(A)**

- A **bar code** is made up of vertical black lines of different widths.

- The bar code represents, among other things, the **product code.**

- To read the data represented by the bar code, a **bar-code reader** is used.

- A bar-code reader is the same as a scanner, but due to the simple nature of the bar code, the scanning is very quick; however, if the bar code is damaged, the code has to be keyed in by hand.

- Bar-code scanners are commonly used at checkouts in supermarkets, warehouses and some libraries.

1.9 reading bar codes

➪ Optical Mark Reader (OMR) **FC(O)**

- An **optical mark reader** (OMR) is similar to a bar-code reader, but this reader uses an infra-red beam to scan pencil marks.

- OMRs are used with specially prepared paper-based forms such as lottery tickets, university student registration forms and multiple-choice examination answer sheets.

- A mark is made in a box to represent a number or letter; the mark is then read by the OMR. It is interpreted by its position on the form.

1.10 OMRs are often used to read multiple-choice answer sheets.

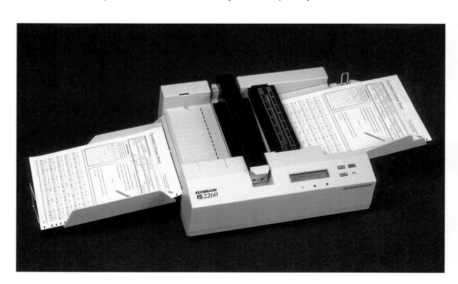

➡ Optical Character Reader (OCR) `FC(A)`

- **Optical character readers** (OCRs) scan by taking a photographic image of printed or even handwritten text.

- Special **software** looks at the image, recognises each character by matching it against a set of stored characters, and converts it into a **text file**. This can then be edited using a word processor.

- The post office uses OCRs to detect postcodes on letters at sorting offices.

➡ Magnetic Ink Character Readers (MICR)

- **Magnetic ink character readers** (MICRs) detect **magnetised ink**.

- Banks use magnetised ink to print sort codes and account numbers on cheques. Then magnetised ink is later used to add the amount that the cheque is made out for.

- MICRs are very reliable with very few reading errors, but equipment is expensive and exclusive to banking.

➡ Magnetic Stripe Readers `FC(A)`

- **Magnetic stripes** are found on credit and debit cards. The stripes can store up to 220 characters, making it easy to copy data.

- The card is swiped through a slot in the **magnetic stripe reader**, which detects the magnetically encoded data.

⚡ A* EXTRA

Because it is possible to create fake credit cards with magnetic stripes, new credit cards are being developed where the magnetic stripe is replaced by a microchip.

❓ CHECK YOURSELF QUESTIONS

Q1 State the main advantage of using bar codes and bar-code readers.

Q2 State the difference between OMRs and OCRs.

Q3 Which type of organisation uses MICRs?

Answers are on page 178.

UNIT 2: OUTPUT DEVICES

▰▰▰ Common output devices ▰▰▰

⚡ A* EXTRA

The larger the number of pixels a screen display has, the higher the resolution and the clearer the picture. 'Low resolution' means the picture display has fewer pixels and so is not as clear.

⇨ Monitor

■ A **monitor** looks like a TV screen and is used to display the information from the computer. A common screen size is 15 inches, although designers tend to have larger screens (17 or 21 inches).

■ Monitors are also called **screens** or **Visual Display Units** (VDUs).

■ Some screens are very flat and called **LCD** (liquid crystal display) monitors. They are mostly used for laptops.

■ Each dot on the screen is called a **pixel**.

1.11 *Monitors can range from high-tech to basic screens for text-only display.*

1.12 *an inkjet printer*

⇨ Printers

■ Printers are used to produce hard-copy output of screen images, usually onto paper.

■ The three main types of printer are:
  • dot matrix • inkjet • laser

■ **Dot-matrix printers** are noisy because a set of steel pins strike an inked ribbon to make a mark on the paper. They are not expensive, and are used when multiple copies need to be printed at once.

■ **Inkjet printers** are also cheap, but they are much quieter. Ink cartridges are used, and the ink is fired through tiny holes to make marks on the paper. They can be black only or colour.

■ **Laser printers** work like photocopiers. They use toner cartridges, which contain ink powder. This is fused onto the paper using heat and pressure. They are silent, fast and used for professional printouts.

⚡ A* EXTRA

Laser printers are getting much cheaper to buy, and a black-and-white laser printer can now be bought for around the same price as a colour inkjet printer.

QUESTION SPOTTER

You may be asked which is the fastest, quietest or even cheapest type of printer. Make sure you know which is which!

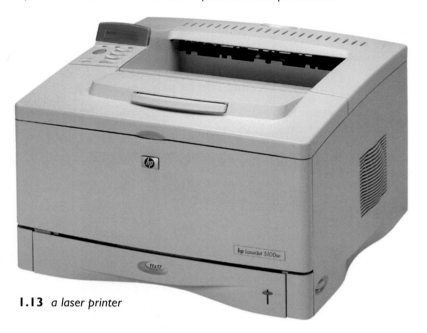

1.13 *a laser printer*

1.14 *Many computers now come with external speakers as standard.*

⇨ Speakers and headphones

■ **Speakers** are used to output sound from computer systems; they are particularly useful for presentations.

■ They can be built into the computer, especially if it is a laptop, or they can be added externally as an extra device.

■ **Headphones** are also attached as a personal set of speakers. They usually plug into a socket and have their own volume control.

CHECK YOURSELF QUESTIONS

Q1 What is the monitor used for?

Q2 Which printer is very noisy?

Q3 Which printer is the fastest and quietest?

Q4 What is a speaker useful for?

Answers are on page 178.

Other output devices

⇨ Plotter

- A **plotter** is an output device which uses coloured pens controlled by the computer to draw line diagrams on paper.

- It is used for drawings where **accuracy** is required, such as building plans and printed circuit boards.

1.15 *a plotter*

1.16 *Traffic lights are usually controlled by switches.*

⇨ Switches and motors FC(A)

- A computer can be programmed very easily to turn **switches** on and off at the required times, for example to control traffic lights.

- **Electric motors** can also be controlled by a computer, for example those found in a robot arm or used to open and close car-park barriers.

- Motors in control systems are sometimes called **actuators**.

? CHECK YOURSELF QUESTIONS

Q1 What is the main advantage of using a plotter for line diagrams?

Q2 Where would you expect to find a motor?

Answers are on page 178.

UNIT 3: COMPUTER SYSTEMS HARDWARE

Inside the computer

⇨ Main hardware parts

■ The main hardware parts of a computer are as follows:

• **CPU (Central Processing Unit)**
This makes the computer work, controlling all the step-by-step instructions and actions of the computer.

• **Backing storage**
This is all the extra storage needed by the computer to store programs and data. Examples are hard disks and floppy disks.

• **Internal memory**
This holds the current set of instructions and data that the computer is working on.

• **Output devices**
The monitor and printer are the two output devices usually attached to the computer.

• **Input devices**
The keyboard and mouse are the two input devices usually attached to the computer.

⇨ Internal Memory

■ There are two types of internal memory: **RAM** and **ROM**.
• RAM is **Random–Access Memory**. It cannot remember any items if the computer is switched off.
• ROM is **Read–Only Memory**. This has the instructions necessary to start up the computer and is never overwritten or deleted.

⇨ Inside the CPU

■ The CPU has a **control unit** and an **arithmetic and logic unit**.
• The control unit is the computer's controller, telling it what happens next.
• The arithmetic and logic unit does all the mathematics, sequences the instructions and works out all the problems.

A* EXTRA

▸ RAM is volatile, which means it cannot save any items when the computer is switched off. It is also small in size, for example 256 megabytes.
▸ A byte stores one character; a megabyte stores one million characters.
▸ RAM, ROM and the CPU work together and are located inside the main computer case. RAM can be upgraded/expanded to make your computer work faster.

1.17 a memory chip

QUESTION SPOTTER

A typical question may involve labelling the diagram of a computer with the correct names of these parts.

CHECK YOURSELF QUESTIONS

Q1 What is the CPU?

Q2 What is the difference between internal memory and backing storage?

Q3 Name two items of backing storage.

Answers are on page 179.

⇨ Desktop microcomputer

- **Desktop microcomputers** are the type found in most small businesses and homes. They have a box containing all the main parts of the computer. This is called the **computer case**.

- The computer case can be placed on or under the desk, and can sit either horizontally or vertically. The latter is known as a **tower case**.

- Desktop microcomputers range in power, but can carry out most small business and home tasks.

- Processing speed is measured in **megahertz** (MHz) or **gigahertz** (GHz). Manufacturers are constantly developing faster processors.

- Desktop computers usually come with standard **programs**, such as **word processors** and **spreadsheets**, although these may only be a 'reduced' version of the software that performs only basic functions.

- Costs range from a few hundred pounds to over a thousand pounds.

1.18 Desktop computers are used for a wide variety of tasks.

1.19 a laptop computer

⇨ Laptop/Notebook

- **Laptop computers** (or **notebook computers**) can have the same power as most desktop computers.

- They are very **compact** and have a **built–in screen**, **keyboard** and **mouse/touchpad**.

- They usually cost more than a desktop with comparable power.

- They are built to be carried around and so are not easily broken.

⇨ Minicomputer **FC(A)**

- **Minicomputers** have a larger-size case than desktop computers and usually have equivalent or slightly better processing power.

- They are used typically by supermarkets or department stores.

- They cost £10,000 upwards.

⇨ Mainframe computer FC

- **Mainframe computers** are large in size – they can sometimes fill a whole room.

- They are used by large businesses and organisations, like banks and building societies.

1.20 *Mainframe computers can fill a whole room.*

⇨ Supercomputers FC(O)

- **Supercomputers** are very large-scale machines which can fill a whole floor of a building.

- They are used by the Ministry of Defence and the Weather Centre.

- They cost millions of pounds.

- They operate at significantly faster speeds than a mainframe computer.

CHECK YOURSELF QUESTIONS

Q1 State two differences between a laptop and a desktop computer.

Q2 What sort of computer is used by the Weather Centre?

Answers are on page 179.

UNIT 4: STORAGE

Internal memory FC(O)

A* EXTRA

▸ All data is stored in the memory in binary form, i.e. as 0s and 1s – this is known as the binary number system.
▸ The program instructions stored in ROM, which make the computer work, are called the 'bootstrap loader'. They tell the computer to load a special program called the 'operating system'. The operating system controls the working of the computer.

QUESTION SPOTTER

▸ A typical question may ask you to state the difference between the two types of memory.
▸ You could also be asked what RAM and ROM stand for.

⇨ Random-Access Memory (RAM)

■ **Random-Access Memory** (RAM) is stored on a chip inside the computer.

■ RAM is volatile, which means that everything is lost from this memory when the computer is turned off.

■ RAM is essential to make the computer work – it stores items you are currently working with on your computer.

■ Some programs need lots of RAM – a typical desktop computer has 512Mb (Megabytes) of RAM.

⇨ Read-Only Memory (ROM)

■ **Read–Only Memory** (ROM) is also stored on a chip, but items stored on it cannot be overwritten.

■ ROM contains essential instructions to ensure the computer switches on properly.

■ Do not confuse ROM with backing storage CD ROMs. ROM is in main, or internal, memory.

CHECK YOURSELF QUESTIONS

Q1 What is RAM?

Q2 What is the purpose of ROM?

Answers are on page 179.

Backing storage

⇨ Floppy disks

- Standard floppy disks can be **high density** or **low density**. High-density (HD) disks can store up to 2Mb of data.

- Floppy disks are portable and can be used on many different machines.

- Floppy disks are known as **magnetic disks** because of the way data is stored.

- They can be either **formatted** or **unformatted**. Unformatted disks need to be formatted before data can be stored on them.

⇨ Hard disks

- **Hard disks** are usually built into the main computer unit, but they can also be installed externally. They are also known as **magnetic disks**.

- Hard disks have a much larger capacity than floppy disks, and can store many Gigabytes of data (1Gb = 1,000 Megabytes).

- Hard disks store all the programs that make the system work.

⇨ Magnetic tape

- Items stored on **magnetic tape** can only be read one after another. In order to get the last item on the tape reel, you must read all the others in front of it.

- In large-scale computer systems, the tape reels look like the reels of film used by the movie industry, but for home computers, the tapes look like music cassette tapes.

- Tape is usually used for taking copies of what is stored on disk.

> **⚡ A* EXTRA**
>
> If you format or reformat a disk, any data previously stored on it will be deleted.

1.21 *Floppy disks are used for back-up storage*

> **⚡ A* EXTRA**
>
> Data is read from both floppy and hard disks using moveable disk-read heads. This means data can be fetched from anywhere on the disk without reading other items first.

⇨ CD-R, CD-RW and CD-ROM FC

- **CDs**, or **compact disks**, are known as **optical disks** because they are read by a laser beam. There are three main types:
  - **CD-Rs** allow you to write to them once and then read them.
  - **CD-RWs** allow you to write to them many times and read them.
  - **CD-ROMs** allow you to only read the data, so they are good for reference material.

- CDs can store up to 650 Mb of data.

- CDs are portable, light and easy to use.

1.22 CDs are a cheap and easy way of storing and transferring data.

⇨ Digital Versatile Disks (DVD) FC

- **DVDs** are a relatively new type of disk; they are also **optical disks**.

- They can store up to 5Gb of data, so they are used for storing digitally produced films.

- There are DVD ROM and DVD RAM systems which are used in computers.

☀ QUESTION SPOTTER

A typical question may ask about the type of storage device used for storing a multimedia encyclopaedia, or for a regularly updated database. You will need to consider the size of the disk, its portability and whether it is Read Only when answering this type of question.

1.23 DVDs are commonly used for films and computer games.

❓ CHECK YOURSELF QUESTIONS

Q1 Name two types of portable magnetic media.

Q2 What is the difference between a CD-RW and a CD-ROM?

Q3 Name two storage items that you could use to store a 500Mb database.

Answers are on page 179.

Unit 5: Linking Computers Together

Computers communicating

⇨ Standalone computer

- A **standalone computer** is one which is not connected to any other computer. It has no special hardware to allow it to talk to other computers or exchange data with other computers. It can only have other devices like printers and scanners attached to it.

⇨ Networked computer **FC(A)**

- A **networked computer** has added hardware and software to allow it to communicate and exchange data with at least one other computer.

- The following extra equipment is required to allow one computer to communicate with another:
  - **cable**
  - **network card**
  - **software** (a computer program)

- Sometimes computers communicate with other computers over the Internet. In this case, other types of hardware and cable are needed.

⇨ Types of cable used for communicating

- **Fibre–optic cables** use glass fibre to transmit data as streams of light.

- **Wire cable** has metal strands, sometimes twisted together, to transmit data as electrical pulses.

⇨ Other ways to transmit data **FC(A)**

- **Satellites** are sometimes used to transmit data over long distances, for example between continents.

- **Radio waves** or **microwaves** are also used for transmitting data. This is known as **wireless data transmission**.

> **QUESTION SPOTTER**
>
> A typical question may ask for the difference between a standalone computer and a networked computer.

> **A* EXTRA**
>
> Computers use cables to communicate with printers, too, but sometimes they can use wireless data transmission. If your printer has an infra-red receiver, it may be possible to print without using a cable.

? CHECK YOURSELF QUESTIONS

Q1 What is a networked computer?

Q2 When might you use satellites to transmit data between two computers?

Q3 Name two types of cable.

Answers are on pages 179–180.

Networks

⇨ Computer networks

■ A **computer network** is two or more computers connected together.

■ **Networks** usually have one larger computer called a **file server** controlling them. The file server stores all the data and programs that everyone uses.

■ Advantages of networking computers are:

- the ability to **share data** and software, and hardware such as printers

- ease of **communication** with other users on the network, for example by e-mail

- **good security**: users must key in their own user identification (**user-ID**) and **password** before they can get onto the network.

- a user can work out any computer and still gain access to his/her data.

■ Disadvantages of networking computers are:

- it can be **expensive** to set up and run a network because of all the extra hardware and the need to employ a network manager

- **viruses** are spread easily on a network because the computers are all connected

- there is a possibility that **hackers** may break into the network by guessing user-IDs and password.

- if the server goes down, the network is inaccessible.

⇨ LANS and WANS

■ There are two types of network: **Local Area Networks (LAN)** and **Wide Area Networks (WAN)**.

■ The difference between them is that a LAN is spread over a small area, for example at a school, and the WAN is spread over much larger distance, for example across cities.

■ LANs are sometimes connected to a WAN, for example a supermarket may have a LAN with its own file server on its own premises, but all the supermarkets in the chain may be connected to the Head Office main computer, making a WAN.

⇨ Network topologies FC(O)

- **Star topology** is where the cables are connected directly to each computer from the main file server.

- **Ring topology** is where a single cable is laid out as a circle. This means the cable goes from one computer to another until the last computer is connected back to the first one.

- **Bus topology** is where the cable is laid out like a road with computers at the end of little extra cables running at right angles to the main cable.

- The star topology is most expensive, whilst the ring and bus topologies are inexpensive.

- Keeping the network running is easy with the star topology, as each computer has its own cable. The bus topology is also unaffected if one machine is broken, but the ring topology will not work if any of the machines are broken.

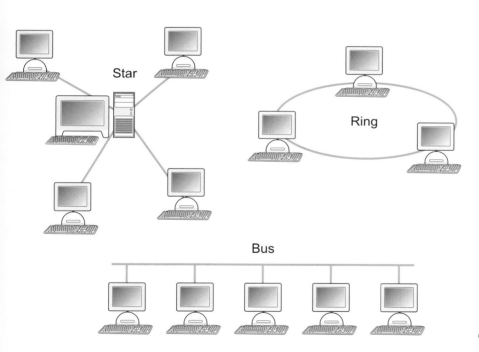

1.24 *different types of network topologies*

? CHECK YOURSELF QUESTIONS

Q1 Give two of the main advantages of using computer networks.

Q2 Name the three network topologies.

Q3 **a** What is a LAN?

b What is a WAN?

c State the factor which distinguishes the difference between a LAN and WAN.

Answers are on page 180.

UNIT 6: LEGAL ISSUES

Copyright and misuse

⇨ Copyright **FC(A)**

- Computer programs should not be copied or used without a **licence**.

- When a program (software) is bought, it is issued with a licence. Unless a **site licence** is bought for a whole organisation, such as a school, each computer which has the software installed must have its own licence.

⇨ Computer misuse **FC(O)**

- There is a law to stop people using computers for spreading viruses, hacking and committing other computer crimes. The law is called the **Computer Misuse Act 1990**.

- The Computer Misuse Act mainly covers:

  - **Hacking** (deliberately breaking into someone's computer to look at, change, delete or steal data)

  - deliberately spreading **viruses** (computer programs which can cause damage to programs and data stored on a computer)

  - **Electronic fraud** (when someone uses the computer to steal or trick someone out of money)

  - **Software piracy** (when someone steals software and uses it without a licence). The copyright law which covers paper documents also covers this crime.

- Anyone who uses a computer which does not belong to them for any activity for which permission has not been granted is also not complying with the Computer Misuse Act 1990. An example may be an employee using their work computer for playing games.

CHECK YOURSELF QUESTIONS

Q1 What is a site licence?

Q2 What is 'hacking'?

Q3 Name two items other than hacking covered by the Computer Misuse Act 1990.

Answers are on page 180.

Data Protection Act FC(O)

History of the Data Protection Act

- The **Data Protection Act** was passed to help control data collected, processed and stored about **data subjects**. Data subjects can be individual people or groups of people.

- The Act was first enforced in **1984**, then updated in **1998** to give new rights to data subjects.

- The 1998 Act also covers a wider range of data, including paper records.

Notification

- Unless they are exempt, anyone storing and processing data must notify the **Data Protection Commissioner (DPC)**.

- Notification is done using forms, and certain information must be included:

  - the name of the **data controller** (the person responsible for data held and processed by the organisation)

  - the name and address of the organisation using the data

  - a description of the data and the purpose for processing the data

  - a description of whom the data controller intends to allow to receive processed data.

> **⚡ A* EXTRA**
>
> The main difference between the 1984 Act and the 1998 Act is that the latter covers a wider range of data, including paper records and the Internet. The new Act was created to standardise the law across Europe, to cover this wider range of data and also to give new rights to data subjects.

Principles of the Act

- There are eight principles (sometimes referred to as the Responsibility of the Data User):

  1 Data must be obtained and processed fairly and lawfully.

  2 Data must be held and processed for registered purpose(s).

  3 Data should be relevant and not excessive to the purpose.

  4 Data should be kept safe and secure.

  5 Data must be accurate and up to date.

  6 Data must not be kept longer than necessary.

  7 Data must be processed according to the rights of the data subject.

  8 Data cannot be transferred out of the European Union (EU).

QUESTION SPOTTER

▸ A typical question could focus on a company and how it is processing data, asking you to comment whether they are complying with the Act. Make sure you know the eight principles to answer this type of question.
▸ You may also be asked about notification and what details are given to the DPC.
▸ Exemptions from the Act could also be targeted.

▷ Rights of data subjects

■ There are seven rights:

1 Rights of access, meaning a data subject can see what data is stored about them.

2 Right to request correction/destruction of inaccurate data.

3 Right to prevent processing of data which might cause personal distress.

4 Right to prevent processing of data for direct marketing.

5 Right to compensation if any distress is caused.

6 Right to prevent automated decision-making based on data stored.

7 Right to ask the DPC to investigate that data is being processed according to the Act.

▷ Exemptions

■ There are six exemptions from the 1998 Act:

1 Tax records and tax collection

2 Crime records, for detection and prevention of crime

3 National Security data, for example Ministry of Defence records

4 Domestic and home use of data, e.g. home budgeting

5 For reasons of ensuring an organisation or people carry out their business according to membership rules

6 Artistic, literary, historical, statistical or research purposes, for example, census data

CHECK YOURSELF QUESTIONS

Q1 State the two dates of the Data Protection Act.

Q2 What is the difference between a Data Controller and Data Protection Commissioner (DPC)?

Q3 List the eight key phrases relating to the eight principles of the Act.

Q4 List the exemptions from the Act.

Answers are on page 180.

UNIT 7: SOCIAL ISSUES

 Computers in everyday life

⇨ Advantages

- There are many advantages to using ICT In our everyday lives:

  - The **Internet** makes home shopping easier for the disabled or people with an illness.

  - Many domestic appliances have been modernised, with **microprocessors** now embedded as part of their design. This saves time and effort. Examples are dishwashers, central-heating systems and burglar alarms.

  - Large companies and government offices use computers to keep accurate records so that they can monitor accounts more completely.

  - **Bank cards** and **credit cards** have reduced the need to carry cash. Instead computer technology is used to transfer funds from one account to another.

  - **Automatic teller machines (ATMs)** are also available 24 hours a day, seven days a week for easy access to cash and other services.

  - Supermarkets provide a fast service and itemised bills because of the quick scanning of **bar codes** and accurate **stock-control systems**.

⇨ Disadvantages

- There are some disadvantages to the increased use of technology:

  - **Hacking** can cause problems and result in fraud.

  - There are many Internet-related crimes, including fraud; it is also possible to edit and publish photographs so that they represent something false. Some Internet sites also publish pornographic and crime-related products.

  - People become too dependent on computerised systems and cannot manage when they are not available. Imagine what happens when the computer system in a supermarket doesn't work or the ATM is broken.

> **QUESTION SPOTTER**
>
> A typical question about ICT in our everyday lives may focus on the use of the Internet for shopping.

> ⚡ **A* EXTRA**
>
> The disadvantages of ICT are mainly crime related. You will not score a high mark by talking about people becoming lazy and doing nothing because ICT does it all for them. However, you can talk about people becoming dependent on computer systems, such as ATMs.

? CHECK YOURSELF QUESTIONS

Q1 State two advantages of using ICT in supermarkets.

Q2 Give two reasons why shopping on the Internet is hazardous.

Answers are on page 181.

QUESTION SPOTTER

▸ Some questions focus on asking about jobs that have been lost, jobs that have been created and jobs that have changed.

▸ Teleworking is also a possible target question, where you may be asked about either what facilities a teleworker needs or the advantages of teleworking.

➪ At work

■ Computers have affected our lives because they are good at doing boring, repetitive tasks. This has meant:

- a reduced number of clerical staff, as there is less need for filing

- a reduced number of manual workers. Instead, we have robots doing the work

- an increased number of computer specialists, such as computer programers

- changes in jobs such as secretarial work, where it is now necessary to use a computer instead of old equipment like a typewriter, or in design offices where **Computer–Aided Design** (CAD) software is used

- redundancies in certain areas, and some people having to learn new skills

- some people can now work from home using their computer. This is called **teleworking**.

➪ Teleworking

■ Teleworking is sometimes called **telecommuting**.

■ To work from home as a **teleworker**, you need:
- a computer
- e-mail and Internet facilities
- possibly **video–conferencing equipment**
- a telephone connection

■ Advantages for the employee:
- flexible working hours
- no travelling time or costs
- the freedom to live in an area of his/her choice

■ Disadvantages for the employee:
- the distractions of home life
- lack of social contact with colleagues

■ Advantages for the employer:
- reduced heating, lighting and accommodation costs
- a happier workforce

■ Disadvantages for the employer:
- inability to monitor the employees' work closely

? CHECK YOURSELF QUESTIONS

Q1 Name two areas where there have been redundancies due to increased use of ICT.

Q2 Name one job which has changed due to the increased use of ICT.

Q3 State one advantage of teleworking for the employer.

Answers are on page 181.

UNIT 8: HEALTH AND SAFETY

Computers, health and safety

⇨ Health issues

- Do not confuse health matters with safety issues. Generally, health problems do not occur suddenly, but after a period of time.

- Computers can affect our health if we do not take care. Health problems that could occur are:
  - **Repetitive Strain Injury (RSI)**, through continued use of the keyboard
  - **eyestrain**, due to glare from the screen
  - **back problems**, due to not sitting correctly
  - **stress**, through prolonged use of the computer.

- Ways that we can try to prevent health problems:
  - **wrist supports** prevent RSI
  - **diffused lighting**, regular **eyesight checks** and **window blinds** prevent eyestrain
  - **height–adjustable chairs** and **footrests** prevent back problems
  - **regular breaks** every two hours prevent stress and other problems.

⇨ Safety issues

- Be aware of the following safety issues when using computers:

  - Electrical sockets should not be overloaded. Each computer should be plugged into its own socket, not an electrical adapter. This reduces the risk of electrical fires.

  - There should be no trailing electrical wires, which could cause people to trip over them and be injured.

  - There should be no liquids, such as drinks, near computers, as there is the risk of people being electrocuted if the liquids come into contact with the computers.

  - There should be fire extinguishers in the room to ensure that an electrical fire could be put out quickly.

QUESTION SPOTTER

- Questions often ask you to list two health problems and then say how they can be prevented. It is a good idea to use two of the first three in the list here and avoid using stress as an answer.
- Ensure that you answer with the related prevention method and avoid using 'regular breaks' as an answer to all.

A* EXTRA

Black CO_2 fire extinguishers are suitable for electrical fires, *not* the red foam extinguishers, which carry a risk of electrocution.

QUESTION SPOTTER

Questions often ask for a description of two safety issues. They could be part of a question about health issues, so you must be really clear which are health problems and which are safety matters.

CHECK YOURSELF QUESTIONS

Q1 a Name two health problems caused by prolonged use of computers.

b Explain how these two health problems can be prevented.

Q2 Describe two safety measures that could be taken to prevent accidents when using the computer room at school.

Answers are on page 181.

Keeping data safe

> Sorry, you can't come in if you don't know the password.

⇨ Ways to protect data

- Safety of data is very important because data is very valuable.
  There are several ways we can protect our data:
  - backups
  - user-IDs and passwords
  - physical protection
  - encryption
  - virus-checking software.

⇨ Backups

- Taking an extra copy of data regularly in case anything happens to the original data is one way to keep data safe. The copy is called a **backup**.

- Backups must be kept safe by storing them away from the computer in a fireproof safe.

☼ QUESTION SPOTTER

- Questions are often asked about backups and what they are for.
- You may also see a question about cleaning up a disk which has a virus.
- Alternatively, you may be asked about the importance of user-IDs and passwords.

⇨ User-IDs and passwords

- **User–IDs** are a set of characters identifying the user, e.g. BHapol, whilst the **password** is a word usually set by the user to ensure the user is the person they say they are. Passwords should be chosen to be easy to remember but not to guess. They should be changed regularly.

- User-IDs and passwords are used for both network and standalone machines.

- User-IDs and passwords restrict access to the computer system so that someone else, for example a hacker, cannot spoil data.

⇨ Physical protection

- It is possible to have a **physical lock** on the computer to stop people logging on. Alternatively, you can lock away a computer in a room.

⚡ A* EXTRA

Secure Internet sites, such as online banks, use encryption of data.

⇨ Encryption

- **Encryption** is changing data according to specified rules so that no one can read it or make sense of it without knowing the **encryption code**.

- Only a system that can **decode** the data can read it, so encryption is useful when transmitting data over telephone lines or, for example, over the Internet.

- Note that encryption is different to the **encoding of data**.

⇨ Virus-checking software

- **Virus-checking software** is used to keep data safe from viruses which might delete or corrupt it.

- A virus is a computer program which attaches itself to data files and other programs with the aim of destroying data or programs and passing on the virus program to other programs.

- Virus-checking software can detect errors and clean up (or disinfect) disks which have been spoiled by virus programs.

- Viruses can easily be spread over the **Internet** or any other network.

1.25 *Virus-checking software can protect external and internal disks.*

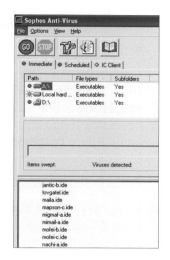

⚡ A* EXTRA

Virus protection software should always be kept up to date to ensure protection against the latest virus.

💡 QUESTION SPOTTER

You will need to know about encryption and physical locks, because you may be asked about methods of protecting the privacy of data other than user-IDs and passwords.

❓ CHECK YOURSELF QUESTIONS

Q1 Say what a backup is and state its purpose.

Q2 Describe one method you would use to clean a virus from a floppy disk.

Q3 Describe two methods of protecting data from hackers.

Answers are on page 181.

REVISION SESSION 1

Batch processing

■ There are different ways we can process our input data. **Batch processing** is one example. This type of processing is used when it is not necessary to process input data immediately. Instead, data is collected and put into **batches**.

⇨ **What does batch processing involve?** FC(O)

■ A typical batch of documents consists of approximately 50 transactions, for example sales orders.

■ Each batch has a slip of paper attached to it called a **batch header**, containing the following information:

- a number to identify the batch

- a count of how many documents/transactions there are in the batch

- a **control total**, which is the total value of the transactions, e.g. the total value of all the orders

- a **hash total**, which is a total of some items on the document. This total has no real value or meaning to anyone, other than to check all orders are present. It could be a total of all the order numbers.

■ Steps involved when processing data in batches:

- Documents are collected over a set period of time until approximately 50 transactions are collected.

- The batch is made up with a batch header.

- The data is **transcribed** (copied from source document to a disk file). The batch header details are also entered, so that the system can make checks on the totals.

- If there is a problem with the batch, it is rejected and checked to ensure no documents are lost or have been transcribed incorrectly. It is then re-input. This step is **verification of data**.

- When the batch totals check is passed, the data is stored with other data on a **transaction file**. It then passes through **validation checks**.

- The data is then sorted so that it can be processed later to update the master file (this is the main file, such as a customer file).

- Updates to the master file are run periodically, sometimes at the end of a day, sometimes at the end of a week.

- Sometimes there are still errors, due to the fact that a master record is not present for a particular transaction. These transactions are rejected, and an error report is produced.

▷ When we use batch processing **FC**

■ We use batch processing when:

- There is no need to have very up-to-date data stored on the master file.

- There are large volumes of data to be processed.

- There are a large number of master records on the master file which could have a matched transaction record on the transaction file. This is sometimes called a **high hit rate**.

■ Examples of batch processing systems are:

- updating customer bank accounts at the end of every day with cheques, deposits and bank-card debits

- weekly or monthly payroll systems where an employee's pay record is updated with their pay for the week or month.

▷ Verification and validation **FC(O)**

■ **Verification** is when we check that what is on the source document is transferred accurately to a computer's disk transaction file. In batch systems, this is done as double entry: two operators type up the same document, and the system check they are the same. In small systems, verification may be carried out as a visual check.

■ **Validation** is when the system software checks to ensure that data being entered is reasonable. Examples are:

- **presence check**: some specified fields must be present

- **range check**: a check that the contents of the field lies between two values

- **check-digit check**: where a calculation is applied to the contents of a field to produce an extra digit which is added to the end of the current set of digits, e.g. customer number 3456 could become 34561, where 1 is the check digit.

⚡ A* EXTRA

Online processing is often combined with regular batch-processing runs to keep files fairly up to date. An example is updating bank accounts overnight in batch mode and allowing online access to accounts for information each day.

▷ Online processing

■ The term **online** means we can access information from another computer that we are connected to. This does not necessarily mean we can update data, but we can look at data. To update data immediately, we need a real-time system (see below).

■ We often say we are online when connected to the Internet. This means our own computer is connected to our **Internet Service Provider's (ISP)** computer over a telecommunications line.

■ Online systems don't always allow for master files on the computer to be updated immediately.

▷ When we use online processing

■ We us online processing when:

- we need to access information from the computer system we are connected to

- we don't need information to be updated every second, but it does need to be reasonably up to date

💡 QUESTION SPOTTER

▶ Control-system questions (see Unit 13, page 44) often contain a section about real-time systems.

▶ The characteristics of real-time systems are sometimes tested.

▶ Some questions may ask you to identify the type of processing for a given system.

▷ Real-time processing systems

■ Processing data in **real time** requires connection to a computer capable of carrying out the processing immediately, so you need to be online.

■ **Real-time systems** must be up to date every second, so the system is always online with data flowing freely all the time.

■ Both input and output data are processed immediately.

■ A real-time system is never **offline**.

■ Control systems, like greenhouse environment control, central-heating systems, heart monitors, some defence systems are all example of real time systems. Sensors constantly feed data to a control system, and this data is processed immediately so that the system can respond.

? CHECK YOURSELF QUESTIONS

Q1 Why is it important for a control system to operate as a real-time system?

Q2 State two characteristics of a real-time system.

Q3 State which mode of processing you would expect to find for the following systems:

    a a heart monitor in an intensive care unit

    b a payroll system

    c an airline seat-booking system

Answers are on page 182.

UNIT 10: SYSTEMS CYCLE

Steps of the systems cycle

- The **systems cycle** is the set of steps necessary to create a computer system from scratch through to when the system is in production and being monitored.

- There are eight steps:

  1 **Project identification**: The problem is identified and described in outline.

  2 **Initial investigation**: You find out about the current system.

  3 **Feasibility study**: You consider whether it is necessary and sensible to create a new system to solve the problem.

  4 **Analysis**: More detailed investigation, (called fact-finding) is carried out using questionnaires and observation, collecting documents and doing interviews. The information is analysed, and user requirements are identified.

  5 **Design**: The new data structures, inputs, outputs and processing are identified.

  6 **Development and testing**: The system is put on the computer and tested.

  7 **Implementation**: The changeover to the new system is decided. It could be that the system is **run in parallel** or **phased**, that **pilot areas** are run, or even that **immediate** or **direct changeover** to the new system is done. Training will be built in at this stage. (See page 31 for details on these types of implementation.)

  8 **Monitoring**: The new operational system is checked for reliability, accuracy and also whether it meets user requirements.

A* EXTRA

- A **user requirements specification** is produced at the end of the analysis step, containing a description of the current system, the problems and also detailing the user requirements.
- A design specification is produced at the end of the design step and contains details of how the data structures are laid out, what input documents/screens look like, what reports and output screens look like and also describing any processing to be done.

QUESTION SPOTTER

- You may be asked to put more common steps of the systems cycle in order.
- You may also be asked about the different methods of collecting information during the analysis step.
- Alternatively, you may be asked about system changeover methods.

CHECK YOURSELF QUESTIONS

Q1 Put the following systems-cycle steps in order: Implementation, Analysis, Design, Development and Testing.

Q2 Describe two methods you would use to investigate a system for monitoring orders.

Q3 State two very different system changeover methods.

Answers are on page 182.

Systems analysis

QUESTION SPOTTER

Most questions will centre around different fact-finding methods.

Just pretend I'm not here.

- **Analysis** is the finding-out and working-out step of the systems cycle (see page 29). It means you look at the *current* system in operation.

⇨ Questionnaires, documents, interviews and observation

- Using **questionnaires** to gather information is advantageous because the person being questioned can answer questions in their own time.

- Questionnaires have the disadvantage that they provide no scope to follow up answers straight away. Sometimes people can't be bothered to fill them in properly.

- **Collecting documents** is useful because it is then possible to interview users about how the documents are used.

- **Interviews** are useful because answers to questions can be followed up straight away, and users tend to offer more useful information.

- Disadvantages of interviews are that they are time consuming, and it is sometimes difficult to arrange a suitable time with the user. Some users are reluctant to give up their time at all.

- It is useful to watch people work; however, you should bear in mind that they may operate differently because they are being watched.

⇨ How to analyse your findings

- Once all the details about data and tasks are gathered together, you need to write up a description of the current system. To do this, you could use **flow diagrams** or text.

- A list of problems and **user requirements** is then compiled to produce a final description of what problems need to be eliminated and what user needs should be met by the new system.

  - Flow diagrams chart the data coming into the system as it passes through different processes until some useful output is produced.

  - Text descriptions are useful, but can be difficult to follow.

  - A problems list is the basis for developing a user requirements list.

  - A user requirements list can be used to produced a detailed **requirements specification**.

? CHECK YOURSELF QUESTIONS

Q1 Why is it important to collect documents used in the current system?

Q2 What is the significance of defining user requirements?

Answers are on pages 182–183.

REVISION SESSION 3 — Systems design, development, testing and implementation

- **Design**, **Development** and **Testing** are the creative part of the systems cycle. **Implementation** is when the system is put into use.

⇨ Design FC(A)

- **Hardware** and **software** are specified in detail, e.g. the minimum size processor, hard disk, memory, printer, monitor and the sort of software that will be needed to develop the system.

- **Input and output designs** (the **user interface**) are drawn up. These are sketched out so that developers know exactly how to make the system easy for the user to use. Consistent layout of screen designs and printed reports with clear instructions are typical examples of what constitute good input and output designs.

- **Data structures** are specified in detail. For example, in a database system, the tables with **field names**, **data types**, **key fields** and any **validation** will be described in detail.

- There will also be a description of how the system should be secured with **passwords** and **backups**.

- These items make up the document known as the **design specification**.

- It is usual to consider a **test strategy** at the design stage, too. This means that a **test plan** should be constructed.

 **A* EXTRA**

The user interface (inputs and outputs) must be tailored to meet the needs of the user. Online help systems, good use of colour, consistent layout, logical placing of items on documents and screens and easy navigation between screens are all good design features.

> I think your user interface needs a bit more work.

⇨ Development

- The design specification is used to develop the system on the computer. This means that all the data structures are set up so that data can be put into the system, all the inputs and outputs are set up and all the security is put in place.

- At the time of development, some basic data will be put into the system according to the specifications of the test plan.

- A **user guide** is produced during the development stage. This provides the user with step-by-step instructions of how to use the system.

- A good user guide will contain:
  - installation instructions
  - pictures of screens (**screen dumps**) and how to use them
  - written instructions
  - how to deal with errors
  - how to take backups and change passwords.

Maybe we should have gone for phased changeover.

⇨ Testing FC(A)

- Testing may be carried out at certain steps during the development stage and also later, when the whole system has been constructed.

- The test plan needs to have enough data to thoroughly test the system, which means a large range of **valid and invalid data** will have been chosen. Test data is classified as normal (typical data), extreme (at the limits of being acceptable) and erroneous (invalid data which should be rejected).

- The test plan will detail what the **expected output** will be for each test run. When testing, the developer must check that the **actual output** matches the **expected output**. If it doesn't, the system must be changed and the test will be run again until the system is fully working.

- **User testing** is also a way to test the system. This means users will try to use the system fully and give feedback about how user friendly the system is.

⇨ Implementation

- There are four ways in which to introduce the system to users:

  1 **Parallel running**: the old system and new system run alongside each other until users feel confident.

  2 **Pilot running**: a small group of users uses the new system first to see whether they encounter any problems.

  3 **Phased changeover**: the system is introduced into some areas of the business step by step until everyone is using the new system.

  4 **Direct changeover**: the old system is abandoned one day and the new system is in use the next day.

- **Training** users is an important part of implementation, so that they feel confident and will use the system properly.

☼ QUESTION SPOTTER

▸ You may be asked a question about changeover from a chosen system, such as a stock-control system.
▸ You could also be asked about steps within the development phase.
▸ Many design questions centre around the user interface and are targeted at the higher grades. Make sure you know what is meant by the term 'user interface'.

❓ CHECK YOURSELF QUESTIONS

Q1 A small store is setting up a computerised stock-control system. Describe the steps involved in the development stage of the system changeover.

Q2 State two features of a good user interface.

Q3 Put the following database development steps in order:

user testing, test according to test plan, set up screens, set up reports, data structures set up, enter test data

Answers are on page 183.

UNIT 11: SYSTEMS SOFTWARE

Operating systems and **FC** user-interface software

■ **Systems software** is the software which runs the computer system, whilst **applications software** is software written so that the user can carry out tasks such as **word processing**. **Operating systems** and **user-interface software** are examples of systems software. Other examples are **translators** and **utilities** (see page 34).

▷ Operating systems

■ The operating system is a set of programs which controls the overall operation of a computer. Without it, the computer would just be a set of circuits and wires.

■ Operating systems schedule tasks on your computer, organise how **main memory (RAM)** is used and decide how items are stored on your hard disk. They also manage data transfers (including transfers to and from peripherals) and manage system security.

■ Sometimes you need to give instructions to the operating system to tell it what you want it to do next. This is done using **commands**.

▷ User-interface software

■ User-interface software makes it easy for the user to give commands to the operating system. Without it, the user would have a black screen with no instructions, just space to type a command (this is known as a command-driven interface).

■ User-interface software allows users to **point and click** with the mouse instead of typing commands.

■ A common way to refer to user-interface software is **GUI** (pronounced 'goo-ee'). This stands for **graphical user interface**.

■ A GUI is a **WIMP environment**. 'WIMP' stands for **Windows, Icons, Menus, Pointers.**

> ### *A* EXTRA*
>
> An example of a command made directly to the operating system is DIR. This will list on the screen all the folders in the current directory in which you are working.

> ### *QUESTION SPOTTER*
>
> ▸ You may be asked what an operating system does.
> ▸ You may also be asked what the features of a GUI are.

? CHECK YOURSELF QUESTIONS

Q1 State two tasks carried out by an operating system.

Q2 State two features of a GUI.

Answers are on page 183.

Translators and utilities

⇨ Translators

■ **Programing languages** such as Pascal, C, BASIC, COBOL and Fortran allow computer programmers to write programs, but the computer cannot understand the program instructions straight away. The instructions have to be changed to **machine code**, which is what the computer can understand.

■ Each different language has its own translator, which converts program instructions to machine code, so there are Pascal translators, C translators, BASIC translators, COBOL translators and Fortran translators.

■ Machine code is made up of 0s and 1s. This is called **binary code**.

⇨ Utilities

■ Utilities systems software carries out common tasks such as **virus checking**, **formatting disks**, **rearranging** the way files are stored on the disk, **sorting** and many other types of general system tasks.

■ Utility software is sometimes provided with the operating system.

■ Utility software carries out all the systems tasks that the operating system does not carry out.

CHECK YOURSELF QUESTIONS

Q1 State the task that a translator carries out.

Q2 Explain what utility software is, and state why a virus checker is known as utility software.

Answers are on page 183.

UNIT 12: BUSINESS APPLICATIONS SOFTWARE

Word processors and desktop publishers

- **Word processors** and **desktop publishers (DTP)** have very similar features. Originally they were designed for very different types of tasks, but today word processors have many new features which used to be found only in desktop-publishing software.

That wasn't quite what I meant when I said "wrap the text".

▷ Word processors

- Word processors are designed to be used for **writing letters, memos, essays, reports, books** and any kind of document where a large quantity of written text can be found. Text automatically 'wordwraps' from the end of one line to the next, without having to press the 'Return' key.

- **Editing** is easy in a word processor: you can easily change text by moving, inserting and deleting.

- **Formatting text**, which is changing the layout or the way text looks, is also easy. Examples are: changing the style of the font (making letters **bold**, **underlining**, making text *italic*) and **aligning** or **justifying** text.

- **Thesaurus** and **spellcheckers** are other common features found in word processors.

- It is also possible to insert **pictures**, **tables** and many other types of objects besides text, but the software is not able to provide the **flexibility** in controlling these that desktop-publishing software can.

▷ Desktop publishers

- Desktop publishing is used for all type of printed material where the layout of different items is important. Examples are **posters**, **business cards**, **leaflets**, **newsletters** and **banners**.

- Every item in a desktop publisher appears in its own **frame** or **box**. For example, text appears in **text frames** and pictures appear in **picture frames**.

- Frames can be **layered**, so that items can be put over the top of each other. If the items are made **semi-transparent**, then it is possible to see several items, even though they are in the same position. An example is placing a text item over the top of a picture so that the picture can be seen.

> ### QUESTION SPOTTER
>
> ▸ You may be asked to match tasks to software.
> ▸ You could also be asked how a desktop publisher could be used to prepare a report in a given area, and how results could be put into the report.

- Items can be **rotated** and **flipped** to give even further flexibility in placing items on a page. Although these features are also available in some word processors, there are limitations in using them compared with the desktop-publishing software.

- All **editing** and **formatting** features can be found in desktop publishers, and you can also **spell check** each text frame separately.

- Each text frame can be **linked** to another for continuation, and sometimes if you put too much text inside a frame, the software will create a new frame for you.

1.26 *Desktop publishers allow images to be flipped.*

❓ CHECK YOURSELF QUESTIONS

Q1 Match the following tasks to the correct software.

A word processor

B desktop publisher

essay, thesis, poster, birthday card, memo, advertising booklet

Q2 A school wishes to publish its sports-day results on a poster. At present, there is some text which has been word-processed describing each event and who took part, a results table stored in a spreadsheet, and also photographs taken by a digital camera of some of the events available for inclusion. Describe how the poster could be created.

Answers are on pages 183–184.

Spreadsheets

- **Spreadsheets** are used for creating **data models**. Data models are numerical representations of a situation. Examples of data models are **financial models** and **supermarket queues**.

⇨ Spreadsheet concepts and terminology

- Spreadsheets are laid out as a **grid** with letters heading the **columns** and numbers labelling the **rows**. Individual **cells** are referenced by the letter of the column and the number of the row they belong to, e.g. A1.

- **Numerical data** or **text** (known as **labels**) can be put into cells.

- **Formulae** (arithmetical calculations) can also be put into cells. All formulae begin with an **equals sign** (=).

- Cells can be **formatted** to change their appearance. Cells can also be **merged**. This is often necessary when text covers more than one column.

- Cell references change when formulae are **replicated**. Replication is when formulae are copied down a column or across a row. If you replicate the formula =A1+10 down column A, the cell reference A1 will change row by row to A2, A3 and so on as the formula is replicated.

- **Absolute cell references** are unaffected by replication. To make a cell reference into an absolute cell reference, place a $ sign in front of the letter and also in front of the number. A1 thus becomes $A$1. This cell reference will now be unchanged by any replication.

- The most common **arithmetic operators** that can be used are **+, −, /, ***, where / is 'divided by' and * is 'multiplied by'. There are also **logical operators** such as **=, >, <**.

- There are functions such as **SUM, AVERAGE, MIN, MAX** and **IF**. A typical formula using SUM looks like this: =SUM(A1:A10). This totals the values represented by A1, A2, etc. through to A10. SUM is sometimes represented by the symbol $\sum$.

- When data changes in any cells, all formulae in the spreadsheet that are linked to that cell will **recalculate** the new value. This allows the user to try out **'what if'** questions.

- **Sorting** in ascending or descending order is possible in spreadsheets.

QUESTION SPOTTER

- ▸ You may be asked to write down formulae to calculate a value in a spreadsheet.
- ▸ You could also be asked to describe a task in a spreadsheet, such as replication.
- ▸ You could also be asked to state the advantages of using spreadsheets for data modelling.

⚡ A* EXTRA

The IF function looks like this: =IF(C1>39, "Pass", "Fail"). This is saying if the value in C1 is greater than 39 then display the word 'Pass' in the cell containing this formula; otherwise display the word 'Fail'. This is useful for working out whether a set of students has passed or failed exams based on the mark they have recorded in cell C1.

❓ CHECK YOURSELF QUESTIONS

Q1 Write down the formula to add together cells C1 and D1, multiplying the result by 100.

Q2 Describe how you would replicate a formula in cell C3 down to cell C20.

Q3 State TWO advantages of using spreadsheets for data modelling.

Answers are on page 184.

■ **Database** software is used for **handling data**. Data is stored so that we can search for items quickly and **filter out** data that is not required.

■ Items you will find in a database:

  • A **field** is an individual data item, such as surname or date of birth.

  • A **record** is a collection of related fields, such as a pupil's record.

  • A **table** contains a collection of related records, for example all the pupil records in a school.

■ A special field is the **key field**. This is the field which uniquely identifies an individual record. An example would be a bank-account number. Two people may have the same name, so a unique account identifier at the bank is the account number.

⇨ Setting up a database

■ First, design the **data structure**. This means deciding on what fields are required, whether you need **validation** on any fields, and what **data types** you need.

■ Examples of data types are **text**, **numeric**, **date**, **boolean** (Yes/No); there may be others, depending on the database software you are using. For some fields, such as text fields, you will need to choose the length, although the software will choose for you if you say nothing.

■ Make sure you have a key field. This may be an extra numeric field or some other field you already have set up.

■ When the design is complete, **enter the data**.

You don't appear to be on my database.

RECEPTION

■ Write **queries** to search for data and filter out any unwanted data using **query criteria**. An example for a pupil record might be: Surname=Jones. This filters out anyone who does not have the surname 'Jones', leaving a list of people who are called 'Jones'.

■ When writing queries, you can ask for data to be **sorted**, too

■ Other items that can be set up are **input forms** and **reports** so that it is easier for people to enter data and read the output.

➪ Query criteria

- When writing queries, you can specify more than one field to filter data, so as well as saying 'Surname=Jones', it is possible to say 'Forename=Rebecca'. This is done using the **AND logical operator** ('Surname=Jones AND Forename=Rebecca'). Only pupils with the name 'Rebecca Jones' will appear on the listed output.

- The other common logical operator is the **OR logical operator**. If you put 'Surname=Jones OR Surname=Brown', this means all pupils with either the surname 'Jones' or the surname 'Brown' will be listed. Note that if you used AND instead of OR for these two surnames, the chances are that you would get no output).

- Remember that as well as the = sign, you can use the < (is less than) or > (is more than) signs when writing query criteria.

QUESTION SPOTTER

▸ You may be asked to list the steps in designing a database.
▸ You could also be asked to state what query criteria are required to get certain data from the database.

❓ CHECK YOURSELF QUESTIONS

Q1 Write down the steps required to set up a database of stock records.

Q2 You have a database of cars which contains the field 'colour', and you want to find all saloon cars which are black, and all saloon cars which are white. Write down the query criteria to find these items.

Answers are on page 184.

Computer-Aided Design (CAD)

QUESTION SPOTTER

You may be asked about the features of CAD packages or what the advantages in using them are.

- **Computer-Aided Design (CAD)** software helps designers to design quickly and efficiently. There are many types of design software packages available, from garden design to architectural design packages.

⇨ How do they work?

- CAD packages allow designers to use **special objects** from a **library**.

- Designers select the objects and place them in the **design window area**.

- Designers can also draw new objects from scratch. These can be saved in a library.

- Objects which are created in a design window are often **created to scale**, and the software makes **calculations** so that objects can become **three-dimensional**. They can then be **rotated** and different views of the designs can be seen and printed out.

⇨ Why CAD is more efficient

- Design objects can be stored and quickly retrieved from a design library if they are to be used over and over again.

- It is easy to edit and change designs rather than having to redraw the whole thing.

- Designs can be easily scaled, and different views can be printed instead of having to draw several views to scale by hand.

CHECK YOURSELF QUESTIONS

Q1 State TWO features of CAD packages.

Q2 Give ONE advantage to an architect in using a CAD package.

Answers are on page 184.

The Internet and e-mail

- The **Internet** and **e-mail** are ways of communicating with others and exchanging information.

⇨ The Internet

- The Internet is an **international network of computers** which provides access to **web pages** with information on them.

- The **World Wide Web (WWW)** is a web of these pages accessible over the Internet.

- To get access to the Internet, your computer must be connected to a **communication line**. This can be via a **digital line**, called an **ISDN line**, or using a piece of hardware called a **modem** connected by a cable to a standard telephone line. Modems change the normal sound signal transmitted on telephone lines to **digital messages** that computers can understand.

- As well as a communication link, you need software called a **browser** to enable you to navigate the Internet.

- You also need to subscribe to an **Internet Service Provider (ISP)**. ISPs have large computers which are linked to other computers, making up the main international network of computers known as the Internet.

- On the Internet, you can **access web pages**, search for information using **search engines**, follow **hyperlinks** to other web pages and do many other things, such as **subscribe** to groups providing news or information or **download information** to your own computer.

- Many web pages contain **hot spots**, which display further information when the cursor is moved over them.

⇨ Web design

- All web pages have to be designed and created, and there is a growing number of IT professionals whose job is to design pages and the software required to import text and pictures.

- Web-design software uses tables to position text and graphics, and allows the creation of hyperlinks.

- Web designers can add information to and liven up a page by including animation and hot spots.

> ⚡ **A* EXTRA**
>
> Remember to stick to what you have covered in your syllabus. Although you may be familiar with other technological 'buzz' words, such as Broadband and ADSL, outside the classroom, you should not refer to them unless you are absolutely sure you know how they work in relation to the standard technology covered in the GCSE syllabus.

⇨ E-mail

- E-mail allows you to **send messages electronically** over the Internet or over a private network.

- To use e-mail, you need an **e-mail address** and an **e-mail software package**.

- With e-mail, messages are sent **person to person** because both you and the person to whom you are sending the message have a **private** address.

- E-mail packages allow you to **attach files**, **reply** to messages, **forward** messages, receive receipts when your mail has been read by the recipient, automatically organise your mail into **folders**, **attach a signature**, store your e-mail addresses in an **address book** and many other features, depending on the e-mail package you are using.

- Sending e-mail is usually very quick, despite the fact it is sometimes sent very long distance. It travels via your ISP's computer to other main computers around the world, then to your recipient's ISP's computer until the person receiving the mail logs on and reads their mail.

QUESTION SPOTTER

▸ You may be asked what hardware and software is needed to connect to the Internet.
▸ You could also be asked the same sort of question about e-mail, or even what features or advantages e-mail has compared with the postal service.

CHECK YOURSELF QUESTIONS

Q1 Describe the hardware and software needed to access the Internet, besides a computer.

Q2 State TWO features of e-mail.

Answers are on pages 184–185.

UNIT 13: DATA LOGGING AND CONTROL

Data logging

■ **Data logging** involves collecting data using sensors. A typical data-logging system is a weather station. It uses sensors to gather data about wind speed, rainfall, hours of sunshine and temperature.

▷ **Features of a data-logging system**

■ Sensors collect **analogue** readings which need to be converted to digital data that the computer can understand. An **analogue-to-digital converter** (ADC) does the conversion.

■ Data-logging systems collect data about the environment and can be used in unsafe or unfriendly environments, such as the Arctic Circle.

■ A sensor may need to be **calibrated** before it is used. Calibration matches the readings from a sensor to an accepted scale in known units.

■ Advantages of data logging:

- Data logging operates continuously without human intervention.

- Fixed and accurate time intervals (**logging intervals**) can be set between readings.

- Data can be collected over long or short periods of time. The logging interval can also be adjusted.

- Accurate readings are taken – no risk of human error.

- Data logging systems can be used when it is not sensible or safe for a human operator to take readings.

■ Examples of sensors are: pressure sensors, humidity sensors, passive infra-red sensors (PIR), light sensors, temperature sensors.

QUESTION SPOTTER

▶ You may be given a description of a situation and asked to name some sensors and how they would be used.
▶ You could also be asked the advantages of using data logging.

CHECK YOURSELF QUESTIONS

Q1 A supermarket wants to count the number of customers coming into the shop each day, and at different periods of the day. This will help them decide how many till operators will be needed. Explain how data logging could help in this situation.

Q2 State TWO advantages of data logging.

Answers are on page 185.

QUESTION SPOTTER

You may be given a control system and asked how it operates.

■ **Control systems** also use sensors to collect data about the environment, but instead of storing the data for later analysis, it is processed immediately so that the system can respond with immediate output.

⇨ Features of control systems

■ These systems operate as **real-time systems**, which means that they process small amounts of input data immediately so that output is produced straight away.

■ These systems have **feedback loops**, which means that the output affects the input.

■ Output can be something simple like activating a switch. There is also an output device known as an **actuator** which can make something happen. An example of an actuator is a motor.

■ Control systems do not require human intervention, but sometimes they are set up to operate in a certain way. An example is a central-heating system. Timers and temperature ranges may be set up. These values are used to compare with readings from sensors. The comparisons determine the output from the system, i.e. whether it is made warmer or cooler.

I wish you operated on a real-time system!

❓ CHECK YOURSELF QUESTIONS

Q1 A greenhouse is going to operate automatically. State TWO sensors you would install and explain how the temperature in the greenhouse is maintained at a constant level.

Answers are on page 185.

UNIT 14: APPLICATIONS

Multimedia systems

■ **Multimedia systems** are those which use a variety of media, such as sound, images, video, text, animation.

■ Typically, multimedia systems are used for presentations, **Computer-Aided Learning** (CAL) and electronic encyclopaedias to make them dynamic and more interesting.

■ Presentations can be controlled by an operator, run automatically for an audience, or worked by individuals sitting at a computer.

■ Each feature can be used for specific effect:

- **Sound** is used to draw the audience's attention to specific activities

- **Images** are used for illustration and added interest

- **Video** is good for demonstrating activities or tasks

- **Text** is used to describe and make points

- **Animation** (moving objects) draws the audience's attention to specific items on the screen.

■ Computer-Aided Learning packages use multimedia to present educational material. They are noted for engaging the learner, i.e. making it more interesting so that the learner pays attention. For example, electronic encyclopaedias use multimedia to present facts in an interesting way.

QUESTION SPOTTER

▶ Higher-grade questions will focus on the advantages and disadvantages of multimedia systems.
▶ Alternatively, there may be a short question about features of multimedia systems compared with printed versions.

⚡ A* EXTRA

CAL uses questions and tests to help the user to learn. The system gives feedback to the user immediately about how well (or not) they are doing.

❓ CHECK YOURSELF QUESTIONS

Q1 Describe TWO advantages of a multimedia encyclopaedia.

Q2 State TWO features of multimedia systems.

Answers are on page 185.

QUESTION SPOTTER

Questions may focus on particular applications and how they work.

■ There are many different applications based on microprocessors. Many of them can be found in the home. All of them require **user input** to govern the way the device operates, and instructions based on the input. The processing then controls the device by initiating or producing output.

⇨ Domestic appliances

■ Washing machines, dishwashers, dryers, microwave ovens, refrigerators and many other modern domestic appliances contain microprocessor technology. This means that a small processor contains instructions programmed onto a printed circuit (called a **chip**) to control the appliance.

■ A washing machine, for example, is automated with several programmes for different types of washing. The user selects the correct programme by pressing switches. This is the **input**, which controls the device.

■ The **processing** is when the instructions on the chip are carried out, controlling parts of the machine.

■ The **output** is when messages are sent to parts of the machine to make them work, for example switch on the heater to heat the water, switch on the water to fill the washing machine or switch on the pump to empty the washing machine. Dishwashers operate in the same way.

1.27 *Many domestic appliances rely on microprocessors to control them.*

■ Microwave ovens also work using timers and programmes. The user input is by pressing items on a keypad. The processing is the monitoring of the time and control of the power level. When the programme is finished, the machine beeps to let the user know; this is another example of output.

■ Refrigerators work by constantly comparing the temperature inside the refrigerator with the temperature selected by the user. The coolant is switched on and off to maintain the correct temperature. The internal temperature is measured using sensors.

⇨ Video recorders and digital telephones

- Video recorders accept input in the form of times and channel selection. Several television programmes can be taped one after another. The system stores user input which again controls switches to initiate the recordings.

- Digital telephones have large memories so that the user can input details of names and telephone numbers. Several functions can often be found on telephones as well as searching the memory for the number required; for example, it is possible to display a caller's name or number on its display.

1.28 *Video recorders use microprocessors to control the timer and record facilities.*

⇨ Central-heating systems and burglar alarms

- User input for a central-heating system is selection of times on and off, whether to have heating and water on or off, room temperature and water temperature.

- Room temperature sensors provide the processor with input necessary to make a comparison with the user input. Similarly, there will be a 24-hour clock running. This will be used to compare the times which have been programmed in by the user. The processor is making these comparisons on a continuous basis, so that output switches can be set as *on* or *off*.

- Burglar-alarm systems also use sensors, such as **passive infra-red sensors** (PIRs), which detect movement in a room, and contact switches to detect when a door or window opens. The user input is concerned with setting the system on or off. Output is an audible alarm and possibly a flashing light.

1.29 *PIRs form part of the input for an alarm system.*

❓ CHECK YOURSELF QUESTIONS

Q1 State TWO sensors a burglar-alarm system uses and describe how they are used.

Q2 Explain how a washing machine uses microprocessor technology.

Answers are on page 185.

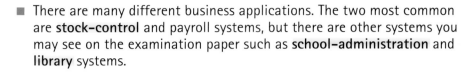

Business applications

QUESTION SPOTTER

Questions about applications will usually be part of other questions about hardware or systems generally.

■ There are many different business applications. The two most common are **stock-control** and payroll systems, but there are other systems you may see on the examination paper such as **school-administration** and **library** systems.

⇨ Stock control and payroll in supermarkets

■ Supermarkets have special tills called **Electronic Point-Of-Sale terminals** (EPOS). These are digital devices which receive data about items sold.

1.30 *EPOS systems use bar codes for system input.*

■ At the EPOS, products have their bar code scanned. Electronic messages are sent to the main computer to read the stock file. The **bar code** has the stock-reference number coded into it.

■ The details are read from the stock file for the item which has just had its bar code scanned. This means that information about price and number in stock are available. The price is printed onto the till receipt, and the number in stock is decreased by the number of items for that code that have been scanned.

■ As stock is decreased for a particular item, the number in stock is compared with a low-stock-level field. If the number in stock is equal to or less than this value, a new order for stock is automatically generated and sent to the supplier in printed form or by e-mail.

■ When stock is received from the supplier, it is added to the current amount in stock.

■ Supermarkets usually pay their staff on a weekly basis. Each week, the payroll program will be run and will produce payslips for each employee showing the number of hours they worked, their rate of pay and the total amount earned. It will also show the deductions, such as tax paid.

■ Input will be a time sheet for each employee showing when they worked and the total number of hours. This, along with their employee number, is input to the system.

■ Each employee's hours are input to the system with the employee code. The employee code is matched to the employee code in the Employees file. The payroll program uses the correct pay rate to calculate the amount to be paid, and creates the payslip. Details of any amounts calculated for the payslip are added to total value for the financial year in the employee's record.

⇨ Library systems

- Library systems **catalogue** and **maintain** files and also **monitor** borrowing and returns. To do this, they need member records and book records.

- Member records contain details about members, not their book lending.

- Book records contain details about books, not who has them out on loan.

- To know who has which books on loan, the system creates another set of data called **loan records**. These records only contain the member number and book number.

- Bar codes on the membership card and book are scanned to create the loan record.

- When a book is returned, the book bar codes are scanned again and the loan records are searched. The loan record is then deleted.

- If a book return is overdue, the reminder is printed from the loans file.

1.31 *Bar codes in library books are used to establish records.*

CHECK YOURSELF QUESTIONS

Q1 In a library system, members return books; explain what happens when the books are scanned.

Q2 State which output is produced by an EPOS in a supermarket.

Answers are on page 186.

 Expert systems FC(O)

■ Expert systems are applications which are written to **advise** or **diagnose** in specialist areas. They contain a large body of knowledge gathered from specialists.

■ Users can ask questions of the system, and it will attempt to answer them or acquire more information so that it can respond with a sensible answer.

■ Expert systems do not have a data structure such as those found in files or databases. They have a **knowledgebase**, which contains facts and rules.

■ The main program, which processes user input, consults the knowledgebase to try and find the correct rules and facts. This program is called an **inference engine**.

■ The user interface is a **question–answer style**, which supports dialogue until an answer is found.

■ Typical examples of expert systems are car fault diagnosis, doctor's advisory systems and tax advisory systems.

CHECK YOURSELF QUESTIONS

Q1 Describe the components of an expert system explaining how the user obtains advice.

Q2 State the steps necessary to create an expert system.

Answers are on page 186.

Short course sample questions and answers

1 Give one reason why it is necessary to verify data when it is entered into a computer. *(1 mark)*

To make sure that it is correct. 0/1

2 State TWO advantages and ONE disadvantage of a school storing pupil records on a computer system rather than using paper records. *(3 marks)*

Advantage 1: It is quicker and easier
Advantage 2: Filing cabinets take up a lot of space.
Disadvantage 1: You need to be trained to use a computer. 1/3

3 **(a)** A school is considering networking its standalone computers, and every user will be issued with a user identification and a password. State TWO ways in which you can keep a password safe. *(2 marks)*

(b) Explain why the password is typed in twice when it is first created.

a) Way 1: Change the password regularly.
*   Way 2: Make sure you write it down somewhere so that you don't forget it.*
b) To make sure that you didn't type it in incorrectly. 1/3

4 State TWO advantages of a school storing pupil records on a computer system rather than using paper records. *(2 marks)*

Advantage 1: Readings will be accurate.
Advantage 2: It won't forget to take the reading. 2/2

EXAMINER'S COMMENTS

1 This answer would gain no marks. Verification can only ensure that what is typed in is the same as what is on the source document. There is no guarantee the contents are correct. A better answer would be: *To check that what is on the source document is the same as what is input to the computer.*

2 This answer would only get a mark for Advantage 2. The first answer is too vague; a better answer would be: *Searching for pupil records on a computer is more efficient than searching manually through all the paper records one by one. The computer is able to show the results of a search on the screen in seconds.* A disadvantage could be that the records could be accessed by a hacker.

3 **(a)** The first answer is correct and would attain a mark, but the second answer is incorrect because if a password is written down somewhere, someone may see it or find it. Instead the answer should have been: *Make sure it is not easy for someone to guess, perhaps including numbers as well as letters.*

(b) This answer is correct, but is too vague and so may well not gain the mark. Give a full explanation, for example: *When you type in the password, you may miss a letter, and so the password would not be what you thought. By typing the same word in twice, you can be sure that is what you intended.*

4 Both answers are vaguely similar, although they would probably attain full marks. However, you could say:
Advantage 1: *Readings taken by data-logging equipment are more accurate, as there is no risk of human error.*
Advantage 2: *Data-logging equipment can be set to operate for long periods of time with readings taken at fixed time intervals.*

5 One reason for using a computer model is that it is cheaper than building the real thing. Give TWO other reasons why it is better to use a computer model rather than building the real thing. *(2 marks)*

Reason 1: It is too time consuming to build the real thing.

Reason 2: It is easier to change.   ½

6 Below is a spreadsheet showing employee overtime and rate of pay. Pay per person and total cost of overtime are calculated.

	A	B	C	D
1	Surname	No. of overtime hours	Overtime pay rate	Pay
2	Foster	6	£8.00	£48.00
3	Parker	10	£10.00	£100.00
4	Brown	5	£6.00	£30.00
5	Jones	7	£6.00	£42.00
6	Elliott	11	£8.00	£88.00
7	Davies	4	£10.00	£40.00
8				
9		Total	£348.00	

a) Name a cell which contains
   i) Value
   ii) Label   *(2 marks)*

b) Write down the formulae used to calculate the values in cells:
   i) D2
   ii) D9   *(2 marks)*

c) Explain how the formulae in column D are replicated.   *(3 marks)*

a) i) Value: B2   2/2
ii) Label: A2
*b) i) D2: =B2*C2*   2/2
ii) D9: =SUM(D2:D7)
c) Copy cell D2 and then paste down the column.   1/3

EXAMINER'S COMMENTS

5 These answers are correct, but the second answer probably would not get a mark. To improve Reason 2, it needs to be expanded as follows: *It is much easier to change data in a computer model and see the effects than to change the real thing.*

6 The answers to part (a) could be any cell from B2 to D7 or C2 to C7, so the answers are correct. The answers to part (b) are also correct. Remember, SUM is a function and not needed for b(i); it totals the cell range you specify as in b(ii). The colon symbol is used to indicate all cells between D2 and D7. For part (c),

only one mark will be awarded for correctly saying you copy cell D2. Other marks are awarded for stating correctly that it is necessary to highlight the cells D3 to D7 (1 mark) and then paste to this highlighted area (1 mark). Alternatively, you can explain that you click on D2, go to the bottom right corner of the cell until the + cursor appears, drag down to D7. The key to answering this question is correctly stating how you fill cells D3 to D7 using the contents of D2, so name the cell references!

7 Discuss the implications of shopping on the Internet. (5 marks)

> People can browse many sites and select items to purchase. They have lots of ³/₅
> choice from many sites. They don't have to leave home and can have items
> delivered to them. The main problem is that when they see the items in real life
> they may not look anything like the item they saw on the Internet, so I think
> it is not as good as going to the shops.

EXAMINER'S COMMENTS

7 This answer would attain marks for: No need to leave home and home delivery (1), wide choice available (1), not being able to view items for real (1) and also a mark for the conclusion. To expand this answer to be sure of full marks, there could be discussion of the use of credit cards over the Internet for payment, the fact that people worry about fraud and also the risk of hacking and fraud. A better conclusion is that it is essential today for disabled or housebound people, although for some purchases people often find it better to go out and shop.

Short course questions to try

1 A student is doing some research for a history project using a CD-ROM and the Internet.

a) Give ONE advantage of using the Internet rather than a CD-ROM. (1 mark)

b) Give ONE advantage of using a CD-ROM rather than the Internet. (1 mark)

2 Describe TWO features you might find on a website, and for each feature, say why it is used. (4 marks)

3 Viruses can sometimes find their way onto the computer.

a) What is a virus? (2 marks)

b) State two ways you can prevent a virus getting onto your computer. (2 marks)

4 An automatic weather station has been set up:

a) State TWO sensors you would use to monitor the weather. (2 marks)

b) Describe what happens to the data once the sensors have read it. (2 marks)

c) State ONE use for the data. (1 mark)

5 Describe THREE ways in which the use of computers might result in increased legal problems. (3 marks)

6 Health and safety matters are a real concern in a school. Fire is one safety hazard. Describe other TWO safety hazards that might arise in a school computer room. (2 marks)

7 Discuss the advantages and disadvantages of using the Internet for online shopping. (8 marks)

Answers are on page 186.

EXAM PRACTICE ○ ○ ○ ○ ○ ○ ○ **53** ○ ○ ○ ○ ○ ○ ○ ○ UNIT 15

Full course sample questions and answers

1 A home worker has a computer at home and wants to send some work to the office. Ring TWO items, which can be used to communicate with the office when working from home.

(2 marks)

midi instrument touch screen mail merge

(telephone) hard disk (modem)

2/2

2 Give ONE difference between a Local Area Network (LAN) and a Wide Area Network (WAN).

(1 mark)

A LAN is a local area network and a WAN is a wide area network. *0/1*

3 Give TWO advantages of using a Graphical User Interface (GUI) compared with a command-driven interface.

(2 marks)

Advantage 1: The user can see things in terms of pictures.
Advantage 2: It is easier to use. *1/2*

4 Describe the steps necessary in developing a brand new expert system from the stage when the system is initially identified as being needed.

(5 marks)

There will have to be an investigation and analysis. Then the system will be designed and put onto the computer. The design will have to have a way for the user to ask questions. *3/5*

EXAMINER'S COMMENTS

1 This can be answered very easily, as the key word 'communicate' guides the answer.

2 Although this statement is correct, it is merely rephrasing the information in the question. The question is really looking to see if the candidate can distinguish the difference, so a mark will not be awarded for an incomplete answer. In addition, the answer should read: *LANs cover a small geographic area, such as a single building or school site, whereas a WAN covers a wide geographic area, such as networks covering a number of small villages.*

3 This answer is only worth one mark, as both are stating parts of the same advantage (i.e. It is easier to use because of its visual look and feel. Items are displayed as graphical objects). Another advantage would be: *Users do not have to learn complex commands; instead they can point and click with the mouse to make things happen.*

4 A mark will be awarded for stating that there will need to be an investigation and analysis, and another for the design – 2 marks in total. The fact that the candidate has mentioned a question-answer style of interface will also gain a mark. However a better answer would state that: *Experts will need to be interviewed (1) to gather expert knowledge. The knowledge would be analysed (1) so that rules and facts are identified. (1) These rules and facts would be part of the design of a knowledgebase (1). A question-answer interface will be designed so that the user can state a problem and then give more detail (1).*

5 A company wishes to ensure that they abide by the Data Protection Act. As well as registering with the DPR, identify six other things they must do. *(6 marks)*

> They must make sure that they obtained information legally and that they
> do not hold or disclose data for anything other than the purpose they
> are registered for. Data they hold must also be kept accurate and up to date.   5/6

6 A company has decided to allow employees to work from home using a computer linked to the office. Discuss the implications for the employer and for the employee. *(6 marks)*

> Employee: Flexible hours and being able to stay at home and work is good,
> but there are lots of other things at home, so the work might not get done.
> Employer: The employer will have to buy a computer for the employee, but there
> will be no need to give them an office at work. The space could be used for
> something else. The employer will also have to trust the employee to get the
> work done.   4/6

EXAMINER'S COMMENTS

5 This is quite a good answer. The candidate could also say: *the data should not be kept for longer than necessary (1) and that the data stored should not be excessive to the purpose registered for (1)*. Either of these points will increase the overall mark to full marks for this question.

6 The first part of the answer is good, but would only really gain one mark for the flexibility the employee has. The question implies that the employee is able to stay at home and is not really stating anything new. To elaborate on the implication of being able to stay at home and get more marks, the answer must include reference to the following point: *The employee will not need to travel, so there is less time wasted.*

Another point which could be made would be: *When working from home, there is no chance of discussing work or other matters with colleagues in a face-to-face situation.* This would boost the marks for this part of the question to 3 marks. Talking about home distractions would need much more detail, and since employees are often given specific targets, it is debatable whether this would be an issue. Avoid this type of answer and aim to include clear factual points in your answer.

The second part of the question is answered well and would gain 2 marks for the two points made in the first sentence. The last sentence would gain the third mark required to get full marks overall for the question.

Normally a 'discuss' question requires a conclusion, but if the paper sets out space for the two discussion points and there is clear distribution of marks for each discussion point, there may be no need to draw a conclusion. However, for good measure, you could add a sentence to state your opinion about home working. It could gain an extra mark if the mark scheme provides for it.

1 Describe the difference between verifying data and validating data when it is put into the computer. *(2 marks)*

2 Which two applications are real-time systems? *(2 marks)*

  a) Printing end-of-year reports
  b) Calculating gas bills
  c) Greenhouse environment control
  d) Processing cheques in a bank.
  e) Driving simulator

3 A small chain of supermarkets runs a computerised stock-control system. The owner of the business wants to upgrade the system, including all the hardware as well as the software.

  a) State TWO possible methods of system changeover the owner could choose from. *(2 marks)*

  b) Describe ONE advantage for each of the methods you have stated. *(2 marks)*

4 A company sends personalised letters to its customers. Describe how they create these letters using mail merging. *(4 marks)*

5 A Computer Aided Learning (CAL) system has been developed and is distributed on a CD-ROM with a printed user manual.

  a) Give TWO reasons why it is sensible to distribute the system on CD-ROM rather than floppy disk. *(2 marks)*

  b) Describe TWO ways in which a CAL system gives feedback to the user. *(2 marks)*

  c) State TWO items you will find in the User Manual. *(2 marks)*

6 The electronic tagging of criminals who have committed minor offences is on trial in a small community. This means that these criminals would not go to prison, but would wear a device for the duration of their sentence. If successful, the tagging device, which fits to the ankle or wrist of the offender, could become a common practice. Discuss the potential advantages and disadvantages of this system. *(5 marks)*

7 A school provides all the staff and pupils with Internet and e-mail access. Discuss the security threats which must be considered and precautions that could be taken to minimise the risks. *(5 marks)*

Answers are on page 187–188.

■ This section covers short-course projects (Project 1A and Project 1B) and the additional Project 2, which is needed if you are doing full-course GCSE. The aim of the section is to give guidance about what you need to include for each project, so that no matter how much work you have done to date on your coursework, before you submit it, you can check it yourself and make sure you have included all the items needed to meet the mark criteria.

■ Project 1A is worth 28 marks, but the majority of the marks can be attained even if you fail to achieve some of the others. There are also marks for writing up general theory, such as virus protection and health and safety matters. Use Section 1 to help you with these topics, as well as the material in this section.

■ Project 1B is also worth 28 marks, and it is important that you realise that higher marks are only available to you if you meet the mark criteria specified at the lower levels. For Project 1B, you can choose the type of project you wish to do. For example, you may choose to do a 'Control' or 'Measuring' project, but this text focuses on the most common project choice of using a spreadsheet for data modelling.

■ Project 2 is a much more substantial piece of work and focuses on practically every step of the systems cycle, so it will help you understand some of the theory needed for your full-course papers.

■ For Project 1A, you need to produce TWO documents to show **consistency** in your design and layout. In this example, there is:
- a poster for advertising school sports day
- a programme of events to inform people about events on the day.

Item to include	Checklist of advice
Collecting information to suit your purpose	Make sure you have collected IT and non-IT materials, e.g. clipart and newspaper cuttings (**text**, **images** and **numbers**) and do a complex search on the Internet. Make sure you find something you can later use in one of your documents. Label where each item came from. Make sure you have evidence of TWO searches. [Extract 1]
Selecting information which is relevant to your purpose	Decide which of the information collected is relevant and say why it is relevant to your purposes. [Extract 2]
Choosing page layout and combining items on your page	Make two page layouts in rough using a desktop publisher, showing where titles, pictures, etc. will be put on the page. Choose the best one and say why. Then take the best layout and talk about placing text over an image for effect. Make sure you have layered text over an image in one of your documents later. [Extracts 3a–b]
Bringing together new information to put in your document	Take an Internet or Encarta image you have chosen and crop it so that you use part of the image in your document rather than all of it. Write what you did to crop the image and where you used it in your document. It could be an image you found on the Internet complex search. [Extract 4]
Deriving new information to put in your document	Make a graph from the numbers you have gathered and write up how you developed the graph. Make sure it is inserted into one of your documents. [Extract 5]
Developing your documents	Print out several stages of your documents to show development. Include text, numbers, your cropped image and an item from your complex search. Reposition text, pictures and numbers. Show 'before' and 'after' printouts. During your development, watch out for any error message. Take screen dumps and note how you handled them. Write about what you did in detail. [Extract 6]
Consistency in your documents	Make sure you develop both your documents to show consistency: same font throughout, same colour title, borders, etc. Write about how you achieved consistency in your work. [Extract 7]
Developing your work to match your purposes	Write about why you developed the work the way you have and why it matches your purposes. Include a comment about why you chose to use an item found using your complex search and write up why the repositioning of items matches your purpose. [Extract 8]
Checking your work is accurate	Check your documents for accuracy. Include evidence of spell-checking and comments from an adult to say it is correct. Include 'before' and 'after' printouts. [Extract 9]
Evidence of saving your work	You need to take screen dumps to show how you saved your work and print them out. [Extract 10]
Advantages and disadvantages of using IT to develop your documents	Write about at least two advantages and disadvantages of using IT to develop your documents. [Extract 11]
Theory	Include a write-up of: 1 two health factors and two safety factors, keeping work safe using backups and care of floppy disks 2 copyright and confidentiality of data 3 error handling and how you obtained help 4 viruses [Extracts 12–15]

I have done two searches. The first was a complex search on the Internet using Yahoo for 'schools AND athletics'. The search results and one of the pages I visited are shown in the screen dumps below. I was looking for mainly images and text. The second search I did was on Encarta CD-ROM, and my screen dumps show a few images I found. I also got some details of top athletes and the times for some typical events for my numbers. I also asked my sports teacher for the details of house points gained by the four different houses at my school.

Coursework Adviser's comments

This extract describes searches and evidence, which are text images and numbers. You should find several items and include most of what you find in your project so that you can later select suitable items to use in your documents. Be sure to follow through with screen dumps showing how you followed your links from one web page to another, as well as the actual items of interest. Use magazines and books as well as old documents and interviews for your non-IT sources, and include these as evidence as well.

I have chosen the Encarta image of an athlete jumping the hurdle because it is full of action and typical of one of the events on sports day. I also decided to include previous sports-day house point scores from my teacher, as they are of interest to spectators and remind pupils of last year's results, and text about the fastest time for the women's 100m and the image of the track from the website www.athletica.com from my complex search, as this is of interest to girls participating in the 100m race.

Coursework Adviser's comments

This extract shows that image, text and numbers must be chosen, along with good reasons for their inclusion. It is a good idea to label all information clearly and to include a discussion of why items are have been rejected.

2.3 EXTRACT 3a
Choosing my layout

Layout 1 shows my first thoughts. It has the title for the sports-day poster at the top of the page, and date and time at the bottom. All my text and numbers are shown above the date. In my second layout, I have put the date and title centrally, and my image of the hurdler from Encarta is placed at the top. All information about the event, such as refreshments available, etc., is placed at the bottom of the poster. Previous scores are to go in as a graph above this text. This second layout is better because it places the main message centrally, and other items, such as an attractive image, catch the eye at the top of the poster. The more informative text follows below.

2.4 EXTRACT 3b
Combining items on my poster

For extra effect, I have added word-art text in the school colours saying 'come and support your daughters and their houses'. This is layered over my clipart image of runners. It attracts people to the event, which is the purpose of the poster. I have also made a programme and used the same clipart image on the back of the four-page programme with the text 'We hope you enjoy your day' underneath it in the same word-art style.

Come and support your daughters and their houses

Coursework Adviser's comments

Extract 3a discusses the choice between two page layouts. Throughout the development of the poster, you should also discuss any change to the layout when you move items around from what you originally decided. Extract 3b also discusses layering text over an image, which is important for acquiring extra marks. The final comment in this extract would be more appropriate when discussing the consistency in the design of your two documents.

Here is the picture of a woman runner that I got from an Internet search [see page 59]. The picture shows lots of background and the whole body of the runner. I only want the expression on the runner's face for my documents, so I am going to crop it. It will create a powerful image to add to both my poster and the programme.

[see page 59]

Coursework Adviser's comments
Extract 4 illustrates how you can document cropping an image. The cropped image should then be put in a document with a 'before' and 'after' printout showing that you have inserted it.

I took the numbers of house points gained by each house last year at sports day and made them into a graph to put on the programme. This gives spectators information about past performance. I put the points for Hunter, Wollaton, Dursley and Tipton given to me by my teacher into a spreadsheet, totalled them and then made a graph.

Hunter	Wollaton	Dursley	Tipton	
68	50	22	91	1st term
67	88	77	77	2nd term
125	120	135	66	3rd term
88	64	85	54	sports day
348	322	319	288	Total

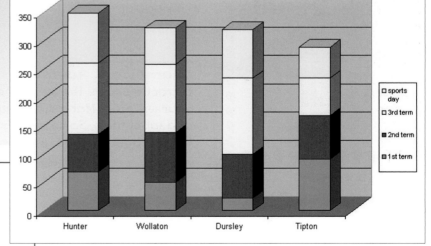

Coursework Adviser's comments
This extract shows that you can derive new information by adding together the three terms' points and then creating a graph of the totals.

printout 6

In my fourth printout of the poster, you can see that I had not yet added my cropped image. In printout 5 of the poster, you can see it has been added. I did this using the Insert menu in Publisher, choosing 'Picture' and then choosing 'From file'. I then looked for my image in my Project 1A folder, double-clicked on the image file and it was inserted into my document. My fifth printout does not have the fancy wording, which I planned to put over the top of the clipart image. I moved the image first, and this is shown in printout 6.

printout 10

When I tried to add text to the text frame which I had edited, I got a warning error message telling me the text would not fit into the frame and asking me if I wanted to create another frame (screen dump 1). I didn't want to do this, so I said 'no', but some of my text disappeared (screen dump 2). I didn't know how to make the text fit, so I asked my teacher and she suggested that I change the font size and increase the text frame slightly. This worked, as you can see on printout 10 of my poster.

Coursework Adviser's comments
Extract 6 shows the level of detail you need to include in your write-up. Make sure you add notes to your printouts and label them. Some evidence (e.g. error messages) will be printouts of what you can see only on the screen.

In my poster and programme, I have chosen a pale-green background for all pages. Both documents have the date and time in Comic Sans font, coloured dark blue, in bold italics, font size 22. The border art of balloons appears on every page.

Coursework Adviser's comments
Extract 7 shows the sort of text you can include when explaining how you achieved consistency.

I chose to use image and text from my complex search in my programme, as I thought the text about the fastest women 100-metre runners and the small image of the track would be of interest to spectators. I put it on the back page, so that girls and parents could read something useful between the events. It will also give girls the chance to see how fast runners can run the 100-metre race. At first, I put these items on the back page, but then I decided to use the track enlarged as a background image over the whole of the centre pages (1 and 2). I then put the image behind the text about times for events. It really gave a professional look to my programme and suited my purpose, as most events on the day were track events.

3.00	Year 7 hurdles final	4 x 100m relays	
3.15	Year 9 100m final	3.30	Year 7
3.20	Year 8 high jump	3.50	Year 8
		4.10	Year 9
		4.30	Year 10
		4.50	Year 11

Coursework Adviser's comments
Extract 8 is all about presenting information appropriately to your audience so that it serves the purpose. This should be the theme of this item. Do not describe how you put the document together in detail. You will have done this in your development write-up.

2.10 EXTRACT 9
Checking my work is accurate

I needed to make sure times, dates and so on were accurate, so I asked the Head of PE to check the poster and programme for this, as well as making sure I had got my house points and other details correct. She signed it to say they were correct (see printout 15 of the poster and printout 22 of the programme). Also on printouts 13 and 14 you will see I have corrected the spelling error found when I put the spell-check on the programme. I had made a typing error in the phrase 'support your dauhters' so I changed it to 'support your daughters'.

Coursework Adviser's comments
As shown in Extract 9, you will need to include evidence of changes due to running an automated spell-check and you will also need to get a responsible adult to verify and sign your documents. Remember to include 'before' and 'after' printouts.

2.11 EXTRACT 10
Evidence of saved work

Coursework Adviser's comments
In Extract 10, you can see the sort of evidence needed to show you have saved your work properly. Make sure that you use sensible names and include several screen dumps of all you have done.

2.12 EXTRACT 11
Advantages and disadvantages of using IT

Advantages: I was able to keep my work organised into a small space on my disks. There were no bits of paper to lose. I could also change my work many times without having to rewrite and redraw the whole document. It was easy to copy from other sources: all I needed to do was copy and paste. Scanning items and selecting portions of pictures was so much easier than cutting out individual items and using glue to stick them onto my documents.

The main disadvantages for me, though, were that on occasion the printer did not work properly, so I could not print out my work straight away, and although the computer did not crash, if it had, there would have been the risk of losing work.

2.13 EXTRACT 12
Health and safety issues

To make sure I protect my health, I adjust the chair I am sitting on to make sure it is at the right height and angle to support my back; I do this at home and at school. I always make sure I shut the blinds if it is a bright day, and I never turn bright overhead lights on. This helps to protect my eyes from getting strained. I always try to take short breaks whenever I work on the computer for a long period of time so that I do not strain my eyes or suffer from tiredness.

At school, we have separate sockets for each plug for electrical safety, and we have fire extinguishers to hand in case of a fire. There are notrailing wires covering the floor that someone could trip over. This helps to keep us safe in the computer room.

I regularly back up my work just in case the original copy is lost or the computer crashes, and to keep my work safe, I also keep my disks and my backup disks in a proper case, away from heat, liquids and magnetic fields.

2.14 EXTRACT 13
Copyright and confidentially

It is illegal to copy software or other items without the permission of the owner of the copyright licence. It is also illegal to use copied software on your computer. I had to be careful to make sure that when I visited some sites on the Internet, I was allowed to copy the information I wanted. Sometimes if you really want to copy something from a web page, you can e-mail the owner of the web page for permission. I did not have to do this for any of my sources.

There is a law that protects people's privacy called the Data Protection Act 1998. If I store details about people on my computer, I must make sure that the data is protected from other people looking at it.

2.15 EXTRACT 14
Error handling and how you obtained help

I had decided to word-process the text I needed and then import it into a text frame. Unfortunately I got an error message saying the import feature was not installed. This meant that there was probably something wrong with the installation of Publisher, so I checked this out and spoke to my teacher, who suggested I use another computer. This time I got a different error message, as shown in my screen dump. Usually there is a help system on most types of software, and all you need to do is search for the item that you need help on. I needed to know about troubleshooting text frames, so while the text frame was highlighted, I typed in 'troubleshooting' so that I could get help with what went wrong. You can see in the screen dumps the steps I went through to solve my problem.

Coursework Adviser's comments
Extract 14 refers to screen dumps. You must show **evidence** of how you handled **errors** as well as writing about them, so don't forget to include them. Include TWO errors you encountered.

2.16 EXTRACT 15
Viruses

To prevent getting a virus on your computer, you could:
- Install virus-checking software to 'disinfect' your files and programs.
- Check floppy disks and your computer regularly.
- Be careful of what you download off the Internet.
- Do not open e-mails if you don't know who they are from.
- Never accept free copies of software.

I tried to keep to these rules to stop getting a virus, as it could destroy my work and spread to other computers.

Coursework Adviser's comments
Extract 15 is a simple explanation of precautions regarding computer viruses. It is easy to get this mark, so make sure you have included this.

UNIT 2 PROJECT 1B

- For Project 1B, there are four different themes you could choose:
  1. handling data: using database software
  2. modelling: using spreadsheet software
  3. measuring: using data-logging software
  4. control: using control software.

- Most students follow the modelling theme as shown in this unit.

Item to include	Advice
Introduction	Write about the user and the business. [Extract 1] Decide which of the information collected is relevant and say why it is relevant to your purposes. [Extract 2]
Choose appropriate software	Make sure you discuss the suitability of two different types of software for building your model. [Extract 2]
Three designs of your model with advantages and disadvantages	Designs should be hand-drawn, and Design 3 should include two mathematical operators and two worksheet functions (not SUM). [Extracts 3a–c]
Put design onto the computer using your chosen software with a detailed write-up	Print out several versions as you put the model onto the computer to show development. [Extract 4] Make detailed notes for your write-up as you go along. [Extract 5]
Make predictions	Write about three 'what if' scenarios and make accurate predictions about the outcome of each scenario. [Extract 6]
Test predictions	Write up exactly what happened when you changed your model to see if your predictions were accurate. [Extract 7]
Evaluation	Write up how good your model is, whether it can be used in real life and also whether the software was easy to use. [Extract 8]

2.17 EXTRACT 1
Introduction

Mrs Jones plans to sell hand-knitted sweaters and wants to make a profit. She will have equipment to buy, and a standard cost and price will give her an idea of when she will break even.

Coursework Adviser's comments
This extract immediately identifies the model as a financial model. Another type of model could be a supermarket queuing model. Keep the business simple.

2.18 EXTRACT 2
Choosing software

... so Model Builder has individual blocks, unlike Excel, which has a grid. Also with Excel, the formulae recalculate the new scenario automatically each time I change the data. This will be really useful for when costs change in my breakeven model for Mrs Jones.

Coursework Adviser's comments
This extract is the end of the summing-up of a comparison between software called Model Builder and spreadsheet software called Excel. Reference is made to the model for Mrs Jones. Prior to this, there should be a list of software features which could be useful for this model.

2.19 EXTRACT 3a
Design 1

Advantage: Very simple – shows the difference between costs and income from sales.
Disadvantage: It is difficult to change items without changing several other things.

	A	B	C	D	E	F
	No of items	Equipment Cost	Cost to make item	Total cost	Sales	Difference
	10	£1000	10.00	=B2+A2*C2	=A2*25	=E2-D2
	20	£1000	10.00	=B3+A3*C3	=A3*25	=E3-D3
	30	£1000	10.00	=B4+A4*C4	=A4*25	=E4-D4

Coursework Adviser's comments
Extract 3a shows a very simple design with formulae calculating total costs for 10, 20 and 30 items. There are three mathematical operators and no functions, so this model is too simple. The notes about advantages and disadvantages give you an idea of what is good and bad about the design. Note the reference to columns A, B, C and rows 1, 2, 3 as found in a spreadsheet.

2.20 EXTRACT 3b
Design 2

Advantage: If one data item changes in this model, other items will automatically change because of the use of absolute cell references and fewer columns.

Disadvantage: There are many different items, not one, and if 25 items were where the breakeven point was, it wouldn't show on this model.

A	B	C	D	E	F
Equipment cost	1000.00	Cost to make item	10.00	Selling price per item	25.00
No of items	**Total cost**	Sales	Difference	Break-even Point	
10	=$B$1+A3*$D$1	=A3*$F$1	=E2-D2	=IF(B3=C3,"Breakeven",)	
20	=$B$1+A4*$D$1	=A4*$F$1	=E3-D3	=IF(B4=C4,"Breakeven",)	
30	=$B$1+A5*$D$1	=A5*$F$1	=E4-D4	=IF(B4=C4,"Breakeven",)	

Coursework Adviser's comments

Extract3b shows a more complex model, which uses absolute cell references and a function to show where the breakeven point is; that is, where the costs equal the sales. Note the advantages and disadvantages have changed.

2.21 EXTRACT 3c
Design 3

Advantage: Now the model shows the average costs of different items more accurately, and the new breakeven column will also show the messages 'profit' and 'loss' displayed in Column E, as well as the breakeven message.
Disadvantage: The average sales price is not calculated.

A	B	C	D	E	F
Equipment cost	1000.00	Cost to make item	=$F$3	Selling price per item	25.00
Jumper design	**Ltwt1**	**Ltwt2**	**Medwt**	**Heavywt**	**Average cost**
Cost	**8.00**	**9.50**	**10.50**	**12.00**	=Average(B3:E3)
No of items	**Total cost**	Sales	Difference	Break-even Point	
10	=$B$1+A3*$D$1	=A3*$F$1	=E2-D2	=IF(B3=C3,"Breakeven",IF(B3>C3,"Loss","Profit"))	
20	=$B$1+A4*$D$1	=A4*$F$1	=E3-D3	=IF(B4=C4,"Breakeven",IF(B4>C4,"Loss","Profit"))	
30	=$B$1+A5*$D$1	=A5*$F$1	=E4-D4	=IF(B5=C5,"Breakeven",IF(B5>C5,"Loss","Profit"))	

Coursework Adviser's comments

Extract 3c is a much more complex model with more accuracy and automation built in. This achieves the important aim of using more than two functions and two mathematical operators, as the function 'average' is now in use.

2.22 EXTRACT 4
Developing the spreadsheet – write-up

I then decided to create an average of the four items that Mrs Jones was going to start her business with. I put the four titles for the jumper design in Row 2. I had to create two rows first. I did this by going to the Insert menu and selecting Rows. In the new second row, I put my text and then in the new third row, I put the costs to make the jumpers. In Cell F3, I was then able to use the function AVERAGE to calculate the average cost to make these jumpers. When I had done this, I changed the 'Cost to make item' (Cell D1) into an absolute cell reference using the new average cost I had created in Cell F3.

Coursework Adviser's comments
This extract shows that you must refer to functions you use and also any other features, such as inserting rows, replication, etc. in your write-up. You should write down everything you did to create your final spreadsheet.

2.23 EXTRACT 5
Spreadsheet

A	B	C	D	E	F
Equipment cost	1000	Cost to make item	=$F$3	Selling price per item	25
Jumper design	Ltwt1	Ltwt2	Medwt	Heavywt	Average cost
Cost	8	9.5	10.5	12	=AVERAGE(B3:E3)
No of items	Total cost	Sales	Difference	Break-even Point	
10	=$B$1+A5*$D$1	=A5*$F$1	=C5-B5	=IF(B5=C5,"Breakeven",IF(B5>C5,"Loss","Profit"))	
20	=$B$1+A6*$D$1	=A6*$F$1	=C6-B6	=IF(B6=C6,"Breakeven",IF(B6>C6,"Loss","Profit"))	
30	=$B$1+A7*$D$1	=A7*$F$1	=C7-B7	=IF(B7=C7,"Breakeven",IF(B7>C7,"Loss","Profit"))	
40	=$B$1+A8*$D$1	=A8*$F$1	=C8-B8	=IF(B8=C8,"Breakeven",IF(B8>C8,"Loss","Profit"))	
50	=$B$1+A9*$D$1	=A9*$F$1	=C9-B9	=IF(B9=C9,"Breakeven",IF(B9>C9,"Loss","Profit"))	
60	=$B$1+A10*$D$1	=A10*$F$1	=C10-B10	=IF(B10=C10,"Breakeven",IF(B10>C10,"Loss","Profit"))	
70	=$B$1+A11*$D$1	=A11*$F$1	=C11-B11	=IF(B11=C11,"Breakeven",IF(B11>C11,"Loss","Profit"))	
80	=$B$1+A12*$D$1	=A12*$F$1	=C12-B12	=IF(B12=C12,"Breakeven",IF(B12>C12,"Loss","Profit"))	
90	=$B$1+A13*$D$1	=A13*$F$1	=C13-B13	=IF(B13=C13,"Breakeven",IF(B13>C13,"Loss","Profit"))	
100	=$B$1+A14*$D$1	=A14*$F$1	=C14-B14	=IF(B14=C14,"Breakeven",IF(B14>C14,"Loss","Profit"))	

Coursework Adviser's comments
This spreadsheet will be your final printout. Print out several copies as you go along. Also, make sure you print out a final copy showing the calculations.

For my second prediction, the scenario is that it could cost more to make the heavyweight jumper, as materials get more expensive. If the cost goes up to £15.00, it will mean that it will take longer for the business to break even and then to see a profit. I estimate that this means that I will need to sell 71 instead of 67 garments to get into profit.

Coursework Adviser's comments
Extract 6 gives you an idea of the accuracy needed when making predictions. You will need to insert new rows to show new values to try as your original model only increases in values of ten. Note that you will need to change other data for other predictions, such as a change in selling price up or down. Your predictions will be based on changing values of data in your cells, unless you plan to change the way your model works.

2.25 EXTRACT 7
Testing my predictions

For my second prediction, I said that if the cost of making a heavyweight jumper goes up to £15.00, it take longer for the business to break even and then to see a profit. I said that I would need to sell 71 garments to get into profit. Printout 2 shows this. I have highlighted the cell (E3) that I changed and added some extra rows to show more accurately the exact point at which the message in Column E changes from 'profit' to 'loss'. My average cost changed to £10.75 as well.

A	B	C	D	E	F
Equipment cost	1000	Cost to make item	10.75	Selling price per item	25
Jumper design	Ltwt1	Ltwt2	Medwt	Heavywt	Average cost
Cost	8	9.5	10.5	15	10.75
No of items	Total cost	Sales	Difference	Break-even Point	
10	1107.5	250	-858	Loss	
20	1215	500	-715	Loss	
30	1322.5	750	-573	Loss	
40	1430	1000	-430	Loss	
50	1537.5	1250	-288	Loss	
60	1645	1500	-145	Loss	
67	1720.3	1675	-45	Loss	
70	1752.5	1750	-2.5	Loss	
71	1763.3	1775	11.8	Profit	
80	1860	2000	140	Profit	
90	1967.5	2250	283	Profit	
100	2075	2500	425	Profit	

Coursework Adviser's comments
Extract 7 illustrates that you must show clearly your results on the printout. You must also state clearly whether your prediction was correct or not.

My model also shows accurately the breakeven point. However, in real life there would probably be more details needed to make the model predict the breakeven point accurately. I would need to include more detail about the costs, as they are very much estimated. The sales of jumpers will also not be the same for each type of jumper, and the average cost assumes this.

The equipment is a fixed cost because it is bought once, so will not be included as part of the variable costs. However, maintenance costs could be built into the variable costs, and this would make my model more realistic and accurate.

I think my choice of software was very good. Excel has a useful Answer Wizard which helped me with my formulae when they were typed in incorrectly. The predictions were easy to do because …

Coursework Adviser's comments
Extract 8 shows two clips from an evaluation. You will need to discuss your model and its good and bad points. Say whether it could be used in real life (probably not) and how you could change it to make it more realistic. Then talk about all the features of the software you used and how useful they were when creating and testing your model.

SESSION 1 ■ Analysis ■

- Analysis is the first stage. The maximum mark you can be awarded is 12.
- Items to include are illustrated in the table below.

Item to include	Advice
Introduction	Write about the user and the business. [Extract 1]
Collect information using one or two of the following: questionnaire, observation, interview or documents	A completed questionnaire provides evidence of your investigation. So do sample documents: choose these methods of collecting information. [Extract 2]
Write up what you found and include evidence	Evidence will be sample documents, e.g. receipts and completed questionnaire
Describe two methods of collecting information you did not use	Describe observation and interview. [Extract 3]
Write good and bad points about the methods you did and did not use to collect information	Give good reasons for not choosing observation and interview. [Extract 3]
Write out a list of problems and requirements	These will follow naturally from your investigation. [Extract 4]
Write about aspects of your system	You should mention software needed for each aspect. [Extract 4]
Make a list of inputs, outputs and processing	Look at data coming into the system and how it is processed to provide useful information. Mention this when writing scenarios.
Suggest hardware and software needed	Events which happen will help you write scenarios. [Extract 5]
Describe some scenarios which use inputs, outputs and processing	Use Internet searches to help you specify an up-to-date machine. Add printers, etc. List features of software needed.
Give alternative hardware and software, then choose the most suitable	Choosing with reasons is important. [Extract 6]

2.27 EXTRACT 1
Introduction

The Petcare veterinary practice has been established for many years.
They have three vets, two nurses and one receptionist.
They have customers who bring a variety of pets for treatment.

Coursework Adviser's comments
This extract immediately identifies the business. More explanation would be needed to identify the users and why it is necessary to investigate the business further.

2.28 EXTRACT 2
Typical questionnaire questions

1 What sort of data do you store about pet owners and their pets?
2 Where do you store this data?
3 Do you have a sample document?

Questionnaire

Please answer the questions in the space allocated and I will collect on the 12th June. Many thanks for your help. David Elliott

1) What sort of data do you store about pet owners and their pets?

2) Where do you store this data?

3) Do you have sample documents I could look at? If so, please attach to this questionnaire and list names and uses of documents below.

4) What happens when a pet is due for vaccination?

5) Do you send reminders to owners?

6) Do you follow up owners when their pets have received treatment? If so, please detail the process below.

7) Do you keep a record of all treatment, visits and costs on each animal record or do you keep costs of treatment with the owner record?

8) What are the main clerical tasks you carry out on a daily basis to keep your records up to date?

9) Are there any particular processes, which you find more time consuming to do than others?

10) Which documents are produced regularly by clerical staff?

Coursework Adviser's comments
This extract includes questions, which can now be expanded to ask about tasks and processes and what their main problems and requirements are. Documents currently in use, like record cards, are needed for evidence.

I could interview the vets, and if they don't answer a question in the way I expected, I could rephrase the question. However, it could be difficult to arrange a suitable time because vets are busy and I may have difficulty writing down the information quickly when they answer. I could also observe the vets as they work, which would be good to see how they carry out tasks and use data, but again as vets are busy, and because the owners are also involved, this is not such a good idea. My questionnaire is going to be the best choice for gathering information, as it will not be too inconvenient for those working at the practice.

Coursework Adviser's comments
This extract briefly discusses information collection methods not used. It could be set out better with bullet points followed by a final statement justifying the choice of questionnaire.

Problems
1 Owner record cards get dirty and bent.
2 Records take a long time to find.
3 It takes ages to write to owners when a vaccination is required.

Requirements
1 A system which can find an owner record straight away.
2 Automatic production of letters to owners.
3 Accurate record-keeping with dates of visits, vaccinations, etc.

Aspects
1 Accurately recording data and storing it safely for later easy searching is necessary for vets and the others working in the practice. For this, I will need a database.
2 Automatically producing letters from details stored on owner records so that vaccination reminders don't get forgotten. For this, I will need a database and word processor.

Owner details	
Name	Joan Barker
Address	16 The Drive, Helstead
Tel. No	9431 686 7511

Animal details	
Name	'Tiddles'
Species/breed	Rottweiler (male)
Colour	Black
Date of birth	15 Sept. 2003

Coursework Adviser's comments
This extract begins the list of problems, requirements and aspects. It is important to write specific problems of the business, not general ones. Note that requirements are directly related to both problems and aspects.

When a new pet is registered with the practice, the owner fills out a form. The receptionist takes details from the form and puts it onto an owner record card. Details include name, address, pet's name, type of animal, pet's DOB. This card is updated each time the owner brings their vet to the practice.

Coursework Adviser's comments
This extract gives one scenario. Think of lots of events that happen and then describe each event as a scenario, but remember to refer to processes and data. Scenarios will sometimes help you identify queries and reports you may need to put into your design later.

2.32 **EXTRACT 6**
Hardware and software

The practice will need a PC with 256Mb RAM, a 50Gb hard disk to store programs and all the data, a 17"-monitor, keyboard, mouse and mono laser printer. They do not need colour printing, but they need quality prints, so I have decided not to use a colour inkjet. They could have a laptop or larger disk, but at this stage they need the data in the practice, and the disk is large enough. They will need a database and word processor rather than a spreadsheet and desktop publisher, as they need to update the database regularly, and it is possible to store data about owners and animals in separate tables. Spreadsheets are better for data modelling and calculations. The word processor is much better than a desktop publisher because the practice can set up a standard letter layout and mail-merge the reminder letters with the data from the database.

Coursework Adviser's comments
This extract talks about the ideal specification for hardware and software. A separate paragraph header for hardware, alternative hardware, software and alternative software, with a final paragraph justifying your choice, will help the person marking the work to see that you have met the mark criteria.

SESSION 2 ◼ Designing the data structure ◼

- Designing the data structure involves putting each data item into a group. Each group will be set up as a table in a database later.

- You will have more than one group. Each group will have a primary key.

- You must do more than one design and choose the best. Each design must have advantages and disadvantages listed.

Item to include	Advice
Design 1	Produce a simple design which has some clear disadvantages. [Extract 1]
Advantages and disadvantage	There should be more advantages than disadvantages. [Extract 2]
Design 2	Split up any fields if necessary and make sure the data types and field lengths are sensible. [Extract 3]
Advantages and disadvantages	By addressing some of your previous disadvantages, your design will have improved, so there should be some clear advantages. [Extract 4]
Design 3	A much improved design that will allow much more flexibility will get you good marks. At this stage, you can include an extra column to show what sort of validation you will put on each field, too, but it is better to wait until you develop your database, as you will also get marks for changes from your chosen design. [Extract 5]
Advantages and disadvantages	Now there will be very few disadvantages, and it makes your choice easy. [Extract 6]
Choose the most suitable design and give reasons for your choice	A choice with REASONS is essential for top marks. [Extract 7]

2.33 EXTRACT 1
Design 1

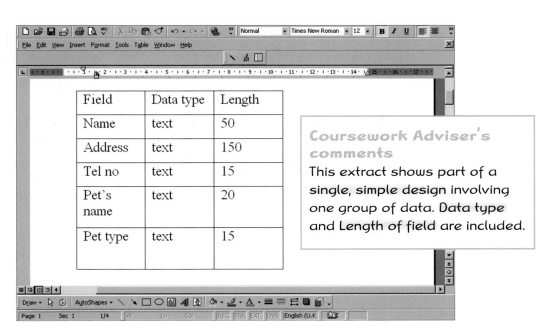

Field	Data type	Length
Name	text	50
Address	text	150
Tel no	text	15
Pet's name	text	20
Pet type	text	15

Coursework Adviser's comments

This extract shows part of a single, simple design involving one group of data. Data type and Length of field are included.

2.34 EXTRACT 2
Advantages and disadvantages

The main advantage is that it is a simple design showing all the main data items found on an owner's record card. However, the disadvantages of this design are that the surname could not be searched for easily, as it is mixed with the rest of the name. The same happens with the address. Really the town and postcode should be separate …

Coursework Adviser's comments
This extract illustrates advantages and disadvantages. It could be improved by being formatted as a **numbered or bulleted list**.

2.35 EXTRACT 3
Design 2

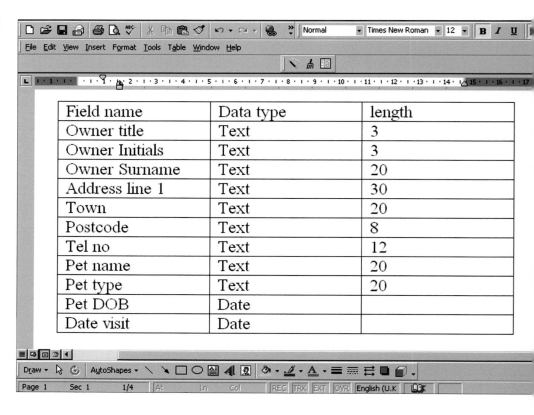

Field name	Data type	length
Owner title	Text	3
Owner Initials	Text	3
Owner Surname	Text	20
Address line 1	Text	30
Town	Text	20
Postcode	Text	8
Tel no	Text	12
Pet name	Text	20
Pet type	Text	20
Pet DOB	Date	
Date visit	Date	

Coursework Adviser's comments
This extract illustrates one way the design could change – by splitting fields and by changing field lengths. There are other changes that could be made, such as coding the pet type and making the field length smaller.

The advantages of being able to sort and search on surname, postcode, town, pet type and visit date make this design very effective. The disadvantages are that this design does not allow an owner to have more than one pet. Pet details could also be expanded.

Coursework Adviser's comments
This extract shows how you can develop an argument for Design 3 being the best choice.

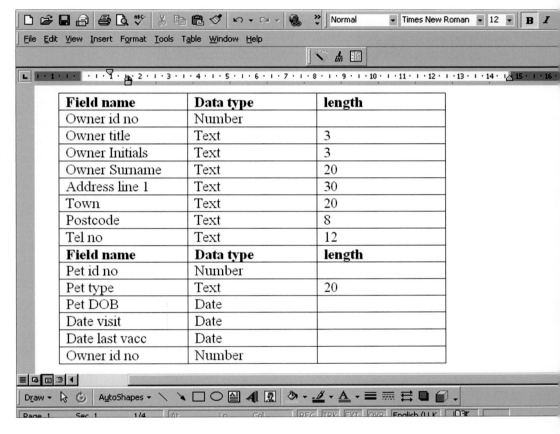

Field name	Data type	length
Owner id no	Number	
Owner title	Text	3
Owner Initials	Text	3
Owner Surname	Text	20
Address line 1	Text	30
Town	Text	20
Postcode	Text	8
Tel no	Text	12
Field name	**Data type**	**length**
Pet id no	Number	
Pet type	Text	20
Pet DOB	Date	
Date visit	Date	
Date last vacc	Date	
Owner id no	Number	

Coursework Adviser's comments
This extract shows that the data is split into two groups and linked by the owner number, so that the owner can have several pets.

2.38 EXTRACT 6
Advantages and disadvantages

The advantage of this design is that the owner can have more than one pet. The pet details are kept separate, and the date of the last vaccination is also included. The disadvantage is that the design is still quite simple, and now there are two groups of data to look after. No validation has been included.

Coursework Adviser's comments
This extract leaves some development work for later, including validation and coding the pet type. Later, you need two changes to the final design. Formatting can also wait until later.

2.39 EXTRACT 7
Choosing the best design

If I had wanted to keep the simplest design, I might have chosen Design 1, but would not easily have been able to sort and search for items. It is also important that the system stores data efficiently, and I did not want a long list of pets at the end of each owner record, so Design 2 would not be good either. Design 3 is much better. It stores data efficiently and allows a variety of sorts and searches to be made.

Coursework Adviser's comments
This extract simply justifies the best choice. You could list reasons with bullet points to emphasise that you have very good reasons for your choice. Make sure you make your reasons clear, even though you have discussed advantages and disadvantages previously.

 **SESSION 3** ■■■ Designing the interface ■■■

■ Designing the interface involves designing the computer screens that will give access to your data structure so that you can add, delete and amend data. These designs MUST be sketched by hand first, rather than relying on computer formatting.

Item to include	Advice
Design 1	Sketch a simple hand-drawn design which has some clear disadvantages. [Extract 1]
Advantages and disadvantage	Write a paragraph about the features of your screen design and say what the advantages and disadvantages are. There should be more advantages than disadvantages. [Extract 2]
Design 2	Sketch a more complex screen design with alternative features. [Extract 3]
Advantages and disadvantages	Write about the features and say which are good and bad. [Extract 4]
Design 3	Your last sketch should be drawn up with more features, and it should also be more pleasing to use. Aim for a very 'user-friendly' design. [Extract 5]
Advantages and disadvantages	Now there will be very few disadvantages, and it makes your choice easy. [Extract 6]
Choose the most suitable design and give reasons for your choice	A choice with REASONS is essential for top marks. [Extract 7]

2.40 EXTRACT 1
Design 1

Owner details
Forename _____
Surname _____
Address Line 1_____
Town _____
Postcode _____
Animal details

_____
_____

Coursework Adviser's comments
This extract shows a simple screen design, with the owner details labelled and a space for a description about any animal details.

The main advantage is that it is a simple design, showing all the main data items found on the owner's record. However, the disadvantages of this design are that the animal details are not split up and they do not match the animal record in Data Structure Design 3. This means it will be difficult to match parts of the animal detail to the animal record. The background is white with a clear title, and the labels clearly identify each owner field.

> **Coursework Adviser's comments**
> This is how you should write about features of the design, and its advantages and disadvantages.

2.42 **EXTRACT 3**
Design 2

> **Coursework Adviser's comments**
> Adding a button and rearranging the text are simple design changes you could make to any screen.

This design has a better colour for the background, as it is easier for the user to look at for long periods of time. All of the owner's fields are on this screen, and they are spread out. There is a button which, when you click on it, opens up a similar style of screen with animal details. Because there can be many animals, you can scroll through a list on the animal screen until you get to the right animal. The disadvantages are that there are no instructions and no way to tell you how to delete, add a new record or just amend data.

2.43 EXTRACT 4
Advantages and disadvantages of Design 2

Coursework Adviser's comments
This extract gives you some idea of how you can **improve** upon your first design.

2.44 EXTRACT 5
Design 3

Owner Details

Forename _____ Surname_____

Street_____

Town _____Postcode_____

Animal

| Add | Delete | Search | Exit |

Fill in the details and press **Add** to create an owner record or click on **Delete** to delete the currently displayed owner

Coursework Adviser's comments
This extract shows that you can now not only go to the animal record, but you can choose other functions, and there are also instructions. You do not need to add all these features to your design. Remember that you will also need to add a similar screen design for the animal screen to make your design complete. Don't just put in one screen design if you need two.

It is now possible to delete, add, search and do other functions. The background is still easy to look at, the animal details are on a separate screen, and the user can easily exit. The user also has instructions, which is very important. However, the design is very basic and boring to look at.

Coursework Adviser's comments

This extract leaves some development work for later, including, perhaps, adding images, more help, etc. Leave your best ideas for when you develop the database. Usually there will be changes because of the limitations of the software, but just in case, save something for later.

If I had wanted to keep the simplest design, I might have chosen Design 1, but would not have been easily able to exit the system or put separate details about animals on the system. Design 2 has a better background, but no instructions, which Design 3 has …

Coursework Adviser's comments

This extract justifies the best choice. You could list reasons with bullet points to emphasise that you have good reasons for your choice. Make sure your reasons are clear, even though you have discussed advantages and disadvantages previously.

SESSION 4 ■■■ Designing the outputs ■■■

- Designing the output involves designing the way your information looks when it has been processed by the computer.

- This session focuses on a report showing all the animals due for a vaccination this month.

- You will probably also need to show a sample mail-merge letter if you want to gain marks for combining information from two software packages. The design of the mail-merge letter is not shown, but the principle is the same.

Item to include	Advice
Design 1	Sketch a simple, hand-drawn design of a report showing a basic layout. [Extract 1]
Advantages and disadvantage	Write a paragraph about the features of the report design and say what the advantages and disadvantages are. There should be more advantages than disadvantages. [Extract 2]
Design 2	Sketch another report design. [Extract 3]
Advantages and disadvantages	Write about the advantages and disadvantages of each. [Extract 4]
Design 3	Your last sketch should be drawn up with a clear layout and easy-to-read format. [Extract 5]
Advantages and disadvantages	Now there will be very few disadvantages and it makes your choice easy. [Extract 6]
Choose the most suitable design and give reasons for your choice	A choice with REASONS is essential for top marks. [Extract 7]

2.47 EXTRACT 1
Design 1

Animals due for vaccination

Animal name_____

Owner's surname _____

Date vaccine due_____

Tel. No._____

Animal name_____

> **Coursework Adviser's comments**
> This extract shows a simple design. You should also show font type, size, colours used, etc.

The main advantage is that most data items required are present, but the data is not ordered to help the user, and there is also the disadvantage that the title does not make it clear whether the list is of animals due for vaccination this week or this month …

Coursework Adviser's comments
These are some advantages and disadvantages you could include. Make sure your design reflects these points.

2.49 EXTRACT 3
Design 2

Animals due for vaccination week commencing 1/5/04

Date _____

Animal name _____

Owner's surname _____

Tel. no. _____

Date etc.………

Coursework Adviser's comments
This extract illustrates one way the design could change. It means you can now talk about having a suitable title and ordering the output in terms of date.

2.50 EXTRACT 4
Advantages and disadvantages

This design has a better title, and the data is sorted by date so that it is easy to ring owners and book an appointment. The disadvantage is that there are no details of the type of animal, and the person ringing up will need to know that.

Coursework Adviser's comments
This extract shows different advantages and disadvantages you can include for Design 2.

Animals due for vaccination week commencing 1/5/04

Date	Animal name	Animal type	Owner's surname	Tel. no.
1/5/03	Molly	Dog	Jones	214679
3/5/03	Suzy	Cat	Brown	136780

Coursework Adviser's comments
This extract shows that it will be easy for the user to work their way through the information effectively. Date order is clearer, and the details are more complete.

2.52 EXTRACT 6
Advantages and disadvantages of Design 3

It is now possible to work easily through the list making appointments. The layout is clear, easy to read and not cluttered, although the owner's title will probably be needed. I could add this into my final report later. I may also make the font larger and the headings stand out more.

Coursework Adviser's comments
This extract leaves some development work for later, but there are clear advantages to make your choice easier.

I've chosen Design 3 because it is much easier to use. It is clear in its layout, and the reader will find it self-explanatory to use …

2.53 EXTRACT 7
Choosing the best design

Coursework Adviser's comments
This extract justifies the best choice. Again, you could summarise what you have said about each design to clearly justify your choice.

SESSION 5 — Hardware and software requirements

- The section on hardware and software requirements must provide some additional detail to what has been done in the Analysis section.

- You will need to include precise requirements, with alternatives discussed and a final choice given. Each item of hardware and software should be named.

Item to include	Advice
Hardware and software choice	Name the hardware and software you believe will be needed. [Extract1]
Alternative choices	Name two alternatives. [Extract 2]
Advantages and disadvantages of respective systems	Discuss advantages and disadvantages. You may choose to put these in a table. [Extract 3]
Choose the best system	A choice with REASONS is essential for top marks. [Extract 4]

2.54 EXTRACT 1
Hardware and software choice

> Viglen's 1.4GHz Pentium is very competitively priced. It has 256MB of RAM, so will be able to run Windows XP and Office XP. This is the software which will allow me to create my database and mail-merge my letters, because it has Access database software and Word for word processing. I also think that an HP PSC 950 inkjet printer with built-in copier and fax would be appropriate …

Coursework Adviser's comments
These alternatives could be discussed in great detail, including prices. Other brands of software could also be discussed.

2.55 EXTRACT 2
Alternative hardware and software

> There is also the possibility of purchasing an RM laptop with a Celeron 1.1GHz processor for the same price as the Viglen. It has the same RAM (256Mb), but a smaller disk of 3Gb. Another alternative would be to buy the Dell Optiplex 1.7GHz machine with 512Mb of RAM and 60Gb disk. I could purchase just Microsoft Access database and Microsoft Word software separately instead of purchasing Office XP, and get a black-and-white printer.

Coursework Adviser's comments
Again, these alternatives could be discussed in more detail, including prices. Other brands of software could also be discussed.

2.56 EXTRACT 3
Advantages and disadvantages

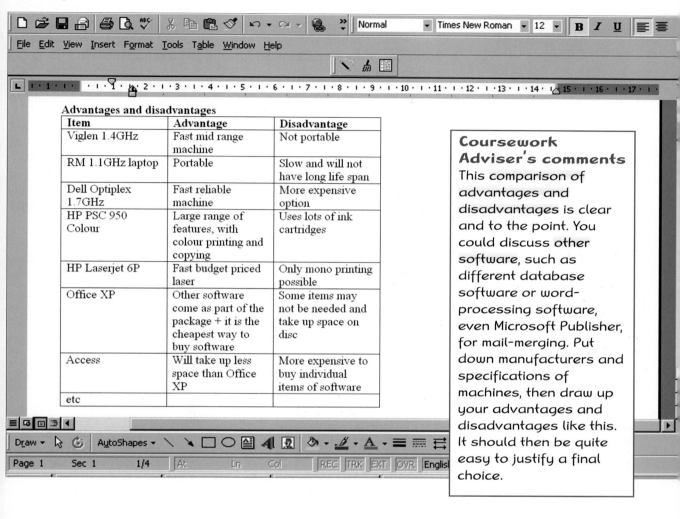

Advantages and disadvantages

Item	Advantage	Disadvantage
Viglen 1.4GHz	Fast mid range machine	Not portable
RM 1.1GHz laptop	Portable	Slow and will not have long life span
Dell Optiplex 1.7GHz	Fast reliable machine	More expensive option
HP PSC 950 Colour	Large range of features, with colour printing and copying	Uses lots of ink cartridges
HP Laserjet 6P	Fast budget priced laser	Only mono printing possible
Office XP	Other software come as part of the package + it is the cheapest way to buy software	Some items may not be needed and take up space on disc
Access	Will take up less space than Office XP	More expensive to buy individual items of software
etc		

Coursework Adviser's comments
This comparison of advantages and disadvantages is clear and to the point. You could discuss other software, such as different database software or word-processing software, even Microsoft Publisher, for mail-merging. Put down manufacturers and specifications of machines, then draw up your advantages and disadvantages like this. It should then be quite easy to justify a final choice.

2.57 EXTRACT 4
Choosing the best system

I have chosen the Viglen machine, as it is more upgradeable than a laptop and is within the price range. The HP LaserJet 6P is also the best choice, as colour printing is not required and there will be sufficient volume for cartridges to be constantly running out. Office XP will provide for all the needs of the veterinary surgery at a reasonable cost.

Coursework Adviser's comments
This extract justifies the best choice of hardware and software. Remember, if you did a good job on the hardware and software in the Analysis part of the work, it should be quite easy to get these marks, simply by naming and pricing items, then following through with the advantages and disadvantages and final choice.

■ Implementing/developing the data structure and inputs and outputs

- Putting your data structure design onto the computer involves using database software.

- At this stage, you will need to make changes to your design. Aim for two different ones (with reasons), such as a change in field length or adding/deleting a field.

- The same principle should be applied to your inputs and outputs. Two changes with good reasons will get you the top marks, although for both data structure and input/outputs, you will also need to write a very good description of how you used the software to put your designs onto the computer.

Item to include	Advice
Detailed description of how you used software to set up your data structure	Talk about the features of the software you used. To do this well, you will need to include a printout of what you have done. [Extract 1]
Write about a minimum of two different changes to your data structure design, with good reasons for the change	Aim for two different TYPES of change, but make sure your reasons are sensible. [Extract 2]
Detailed description of how you used software to set up your inputs and outputs	Talk about the features of the software you used. To do this well, you will need to include a printout of what you have done. [Extract3]
Write about a minimum of two different changes to your input and output designs with good reasons for the change	With the input changes, it may be changing something like the colour or adding a picture. With the output changes, it may be a bigger space for a particular item or a change of font size to make sure items fit where you want them. [Extract 4]

After setting the postcode field to text, I decided to add a mask to make sure that the user could only enter two letters, two numbers, a space and then a number followed by two letters. This feature is very useful for making sure people don't enter silly postcodes. I then set up 'Telephone number' as a number field, and then set 'Owner number' as the key field: another useful feature. I then used Design view to set up my pet table as shown in printout 2. Again, I used the data type, field length and format to set up each field as I wanted them. When I had done this, I set up the relationship between the two tables. I did this by …

Coursework Adviser's comments
Your description should include printout evidence of what you have done, as well as a detailed description of each feature and step you took to set up the data structure.

I added an input mask to control what users entered for the postcode. I did this to ensure that sensible data was added. I also made the 'Pet type' a look-up table so that users do not need to keep typing in the pet type. Instead, they can just choose from the list of pet types. I also added another field to the pet table: 'Reason for last visit'. This is a text field and will be useful for knowing whether the visit was for vaccination or due to illness.

Coursework Adviser's comments
These changes have reasons mentioned, along with the description of the change. You could also draw up a bullet-point list of changes with the reason for each.

2.60 EXTRACT 3
*Setting up my inputs
and outputs*

I used the Form Wizard to set up my input form. It set up the design more or less as I wanted it. I chose the title and background, but there were no buttons to move from one form to another or to add or remove records. I added the buttons as I wanted using the Button Wizard. You can see a screen dump of both the input forms for my owner and pet designs in printouts 4 and 5. In printouts 6 and 7, you can see screen dumps of the Form Wizard and Button Wizard in action.

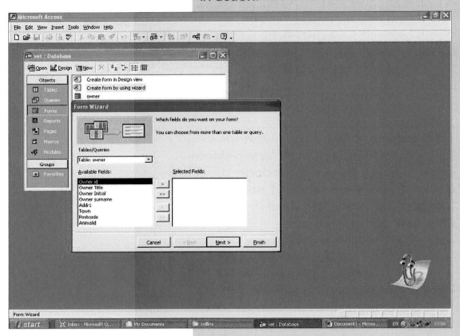

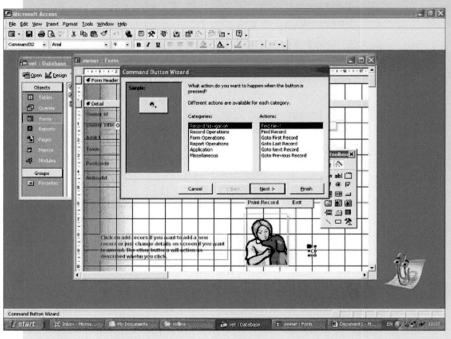

The output showing all the animals due for vaccination is shown in printout 8. I used the Report Wizard for creating this, as shown in the screen dump below. It did not make the report exactly as I wanted, so I had to move some of the fields around a little. I did create a query first in Design view, as shown in the screen dump. I selected the query as the basis for my report. This makes the output from the query go into the report. I was pleased with the result. In the query, I had to set up query criteria. These were …

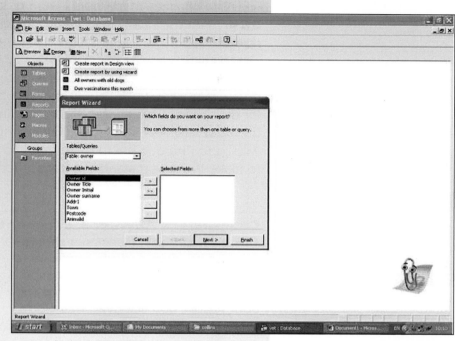

Coursework Adviser's comments
This extract shows two parts of the text where inputs and outputs are briefly described. In this extract, it would be better to put screen dumps in the text, so that you can refer to what happened step by step as you used the query feature, the Report Wizard, the Button Wizard and the Form Wizard. Although it's tedious doing the screen dumps, it saves a lot of writing. Evidence of final screen and reports or query outputs must also be included.

The main changes to my inputs were to include an image, which is a logo for the veterinary surgery. This improves the look of the screens. I also changed the text on the 'Animal' button to read 'Go to animal details'. This is better, as there is no instruction about going to the animal record. I also added a Print button, so that it is possible to print off the current screen details. As there was no title for the owner, I added this. It is important to include this, as then the veterinary receptionist will know whether to ask for 'Mr', 'Mrs', 'Miss', etc. The title is also quite small, so I changed the font size to make the report stand out from other reports.

Coursework Adviser's comments
This extract again discusses changes with justification. Include printouts to show your final report. Remember, if you are using a variety of styles for your report, you will need to include these, as well as details of screen outputs, or even outputs direct from your queries. Also, to get extra marks later, one of your outputs should be a mail-merge letter.

Evidence of software features and other software combined

- For this part of the coursework, you will gain extra marks for combining data from your database into a document created by a different piece of software.

- An easy way to do this is to create a mail-merge letter. As there are two marks for two combined items, it is a good idea to do two different mail-merge letters.

- The rest of the marks for this part of the coursework are for using software features of two different types of software. You will need to briefly summarise this.

Item to include	Advice
A standard mail-merge letter (include two if you want 2 marks instead of 1, and write up how you did your mail merge)	Print out your standard letter [Extract1] and write notes of how you did your mail merge. [Extract 2]
Print out a query you can merge with the standard letter and also the merged letters	Choose a query which produces only one or two items, so that you do not have masses of letters. [Extract 3]
Write about the features of the word processor you used and the features of the database you used, saying WHY you chose to use those features	Make sure you use at least two features of each piece of software. Write about alternative features and justify your choice. [Extract 4]

2.62 EXTRACT I
Standard mail-merge letter

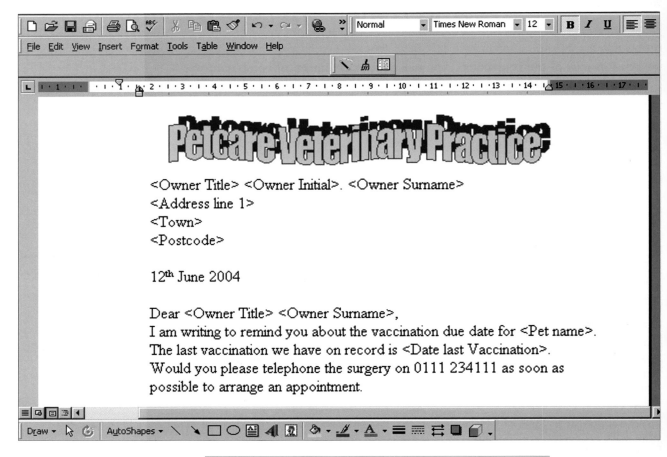

Coursework Adviser's comments
Your letter should clearly show the data items
you are going to merge from your data structure.

2.63 EXTRACT 2
How the standard mail-merge letter was produced

I wrote the letter on my word processor and put the header as a word-art item with the name of the veterinary surgery. I used the spellchecker by clicking on the Tools pull-down menu, then choosing Spelling and grammar. When I was happy with the content of my letter, I clicked on the Tools menu again, but this time I chose the Mail-merge option. I then chose Form letters in the dialogue box and the Get data option. The window displayed did not show my database, so I had to choose Access databases as the file type before I could see it. I selected my database and chose the reminder query.

Coursework Adviser's comments
It is a good idea to print out screen dumps showing steps you took to create your mail-merge letter.

2.64 EXTRACT 3
Results of the due vaccination query

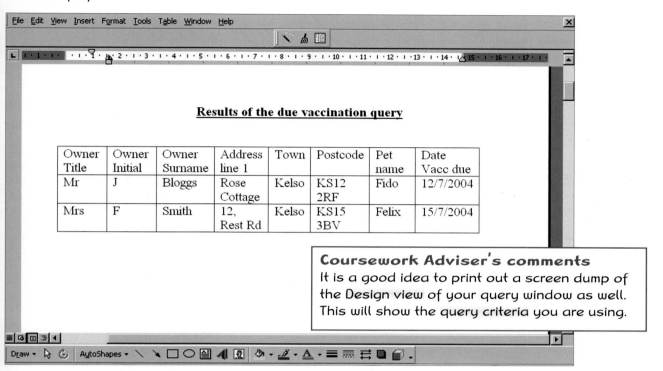

File Edit View Insert Format Tools Table Window Help

Results of the due vaccination query

Owner Title	Owner Initial	Owner Surname	Address line 1	Town	Postcode	Pet name	Date Vacc due
Mr	J	Bloggs	Rose Cottage	Kelso	KS12 2RF	Fido	12/7/2004
Mrs	F	Smith	12, Rest Rd	Kelso	KS15 3BV	Felix	15/7/2004

Coursework Adviser's comments
It is a good idea to print out a screen dump of the Design view of your query window as well. This will show the query criteria you are using.

Draw ▾ AutoShapes ▾

In my database, I also used the Form Wizard to set up my input forms. I could have used Design view and created my forms from scratch, but it was much easier to let the Wizard create the basic form for me to edit as I chose. This saved lots of time. I also chose to create queries, but this time I chose to use the Design view and create the queries from scratch myself, rather than using the Query Wizard. This was because I would have had to edit the query so much; it was better to start from Design view. I also used the Report feature, as my queries all looked very basic and nothing like my output designs.

In my word-processed letters, I used the word-art feature for the veterinary practice name. I could have used standard text, but I thought it looked more professional and eye-catching. I also used the Mail-merge tool to merge in my queries to create customised letters, rather than writing every single letter by editing in each name and address. This again saved lots of time.

2.65 EXTRACT 4
Features of software used and why

Coursework Adviser's comments
This extract shows two parts of the text for the two different software products. Each one clearly discusses features and what they were used for, alternatives and finally justifies the choice. To gain top marks for this part, you must give reasons for choices, as well as talking about the features.

SESSION 8   Testing

- For this part of the coursework, you have to describe your testing, which involves printing your results and getting users to test your system and describe the results.

- You also have to describe the results, which means you will say what you expect your results to be, what they actually turned out to be and why you chose your test data.

Item to include	Advice
A table showing your data, your expected results and actual results, plus an explanation of your choice of data	For full marks, include all methods used to thoroughly test your system. Note the column for printout numbers. [Extract 1] Write about why you chose the set of test data in your table. [Extract 2]
Print out evidence of running each test and write on each one to link it to your test table	Number your printouts and annotate them clearly. [Extract 3]
Include a questionnaire filled in by your users, which will provide evidence that your user has tested the system	Make sure you ask questions about every aspect of your system and how easy your system was to use. [Extract 4]

2.66 EXTRACT 1
Test table showing results

Purpose	Test data	Expected result	Actual result	Printout nos.
To check new owner added	Mr Bloggs	Mr Bloggs added	As expected	1,2
To check pet deleted	Coco	Coco deleted	As expected	3,4
To check vaccination due query for next month	Felix, Fido	Only Felix and Fido should display as they are due in July	As expected	5

Coursework Adviser's comments
Your table will be much more comprehensive than this extract, as you will also need to include validation tests, adding, deleting and amending records from all your tables, all your queries, buttons on screens to see if they work and, of course, your mail merges.

2.67 EXTRACT 2
Explain the choice of test data

I chose my data to ensure thorough testing of every aspect of my system. I included valid and invalid data to make sure error messages appeared when they should. This tested my validation. I tested queries, making sure the right output was produced, and my reports to ensure the format was correct. I used enough data in my tables and chose each item carefully when I wanted to run queries. I added items to all my tables and made sure items would delete, too.

Coursework Adviser's comments
In this extract, the basics have been included. You may want to point out specific examples of data, as this extract is rather general in nature. Remember to include something about your mail merge.

2.68 EXTRACT 3
Results of the due vaccination query

Note that only animals due in July are printed out.

Owner title	Owner initial	Owner surname	Address line 1	Town	Postcode	Pet name	Date/vacc. due
Mr	J	Bloggs	Rose Cottage	Kelso	KS12 2RF	Fido	12/7/2003
Mrs	F	Smith	12, Rest Road	Kelso	KS15 3BV	Felix	15/7/2003

Coursework Adviser's comments
Each printout should be numbered to link to your results table. In some cases, you will need a 'before' and 'after' printout, such as when you add an item to a table. You will need to annotate your printouts to show what has happened. A brief write-up summarising your results and how you achieved them will also make sure you get your message across to the moderator.

2.69 EXTRACT 4
*Part of a questionnaire
filled in by users*

3 Did all the buttons on the screen work properly? Yes/No
  Please include details of any which didn't work in the space below.
  Yes, except for the 'Delete owner'. An error message said I could not delete because there was a linked record in the animal table.

4 Did the two mail merges work as expected?
  Yes, but I think the first mail-merge letter could be improved.
  It needs the opening times of the surgery adding so that people ring up when we are open.

5 Are the report formats as you expected? Do you need any changes?
  Yes, they are perfect and for now no changes are necessary.

Coursework Adviser's comments
This extract shows some typical questions that the user should answer. Make sure that you check that the screen displays (forms) are easy to use. Ask them also to make a note of any unexpected errors or anything they did not like. Finally, make sure you include space for their signature. If possible, get a sentence saying they are pleased with the system. You can later discuss these results in your evaluation.

User documentation

- For this part of the coursework, you have to write a guide to show a user how to enter amend and save data.

- Then you need to show the user how to process and output data and finally how to avoid problems.

Item to include	Advice
Written instructions to show how to add, change and save records in your tables	Include every single step the user must take and use screen dumps to illustrate those steps. [Extract 1]
Written instructions to show how to run queries, mail merges, print reports and display information on the screen	Again, you will need screen dumps, sample printouts and detailed instructions. [Extract 2]
Written instructions about possible errors or problems and how to overcome them	Make sure you include two different errors or problems. [Extract 3]

2.70 EXTRACT 1
Adding, amending and saving data

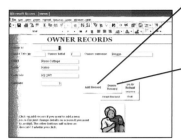

To change the postcode, you just need to click on the postcode field and change it. To add a new record, you just click on the 'Add record' button. Records are automatically saved, so you don't need to do anything other than fill in the boxes on the screen. To delete a record, click on the 'Delete record' button.

Coursework Adviser's comments

This extract is just an example of how detailed you need to make your instructions. You must do this for every different record you add, amend and save. In this case, there are two types of record – animal records and owner records – so similar instructions are required for the animal record. Notice the 'Delete record' button is mentioned, too.

2.71 EXTRACT 2
Processing data and printing information

The screen dump of the owner record also shows buttons for printing an individual record, but by running queries, you can print several records. For example, there is a query to print all the owners who have several animals and a query to print all the animals

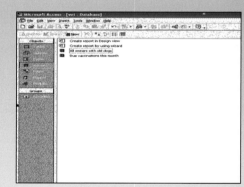

with due vaccinations. Some queries have a much nicer layout, so instead of running the query on its own, you can print a report instead. To do this, go to the main database window as shown in the screen dump below and select 'Reports'. Choose the report you want to print and double click. This will display the report on screen, and then you just need to click on the File menu and print as normal.

Coursework Adviser's comments

In this extract, the basics have been included. You will probably need to add more screen dumps in between your instructions to illustrate steps taken, and you will also want to show ALL queries, screen dumps of ALL reports and how to run ALL your mail merges. Make sure your user instructions are complete, showing all aspects of your system.

3 When you try to delete an owner, an error message may say you cannot delete because there is a linked record in the animal table. You will need to go to the animal table and make sure that these animals for the owner are deleted first. This is a good way of ensuring no owners are deleted when you still have animals on your books.

4 If you get a blank report with no data, don't worry: this usually means that there is no data to display. You can check this by scrolling through the records, but it will take a long time. The system has been tested to ensure the right data is selected, so there should be no need to do this.

5 If you get a message such as 'postcode is invalid' or 'title is invalid' or any other type of message involving invalid data when adding or amending records, please check the table of rules for entering data on the last page of this guide. It just means that you have typed in data not allowed by the system.

Coursework Adviser's comments
Here is an extract showing some problems and how to deal with them. You could also add more general problems, such as how to deal with printer out of paper, duplicate records or any other issue. Four or five problems are plenty! Try and include problems mentioned by your user when filling in your questionnaire.

■ For the Evaluation section of the coursework, you need to write up how well your system meets the needs of your user and how it can be improved.

Item to include	Advice
Copy your user requirements and aspects, then write up which parts of your system meet these requirements	Ensure you write about all the features of your system, including mail-merge letters or any other combined software parts of your solution. [Extract 1]
Explain anything that went wrong and how you could overcome the problems	No system is perfect. Write up what you think you can improve. [Extract 2]
Give user feedback and write up improvements needed to perfect the system from your users' point of view	This part of the evaluation can be quite short, as the questionnaire will speak for itself. [Extract 3]

2.73 EXTRACT 1
Meeting user requirements

The requirements that my user said were needed are:

1 A system which can find an owner record straight away.
I had planned to include a Search button to do this and included it in my design, but I didn't have time to do this part of the system. Instead, the user has to scroll through all the records or run a query to do it.

2 Automatic production of letters to owners.
I managed to do this with my mail-merge facility. I created two mail merges. One was to send a reminder to owners so that they would ring for an appointment to vaccinate their animal when due and …

Aspects of my system I tried to target were:

1 Accurately recording data and storing it safely for later easy searching. This is necessary for vets and the others working in the practice. For this, I will need a database.
I did use a database and created linked tables for animals and owners, so that vets, nurses and receptionists can see all the information at the touch of a button. I also used queries to produce information on screen and in printed format very quickly.

2 Automatically producing letters from details stored on owner records so that vaccination reminders don't get forgotten. For this I will need a database and word processor.
I used a word processor to create a standard letter, then merged a query for vaccination reminders. This created customised letters to individual owners.

Coursework Adviser's comments
The extract here is an example of how you can take your original targets which you wrote about at the end of your Analysis section and explain how you met those targets.

It was very difficult to stick to my design. Some things I would like to have done, but I did not have time to finish; also, the software did not cater for absolutely everything. For example, I wanted to put the veterinary surgery's logo on all reports and letters, but I did not get chance to scan in their chosen design. This can be put in later. I also forgot to include the owner's telephone number, which although I said I needed in my design, it just got left out when I did my data structures.

To improve the way reports work, I could create a screen with just buttons on it to click on and print. At present, users have to go to the reports or queries in the main database window to get information.

When I tested my queries, most worked, but I had to change …

2.74 EXTRACT 2
Collecting information

Coursework Adviser's comments

A very basic extract from this part of the evaluation shows the sort of things you could talk about. Make sure you talk about any errors in your testing, or awkwardness in your design which means users struggle to carry out a particular task.

2.75 EXTRACT 3
Evaluation from the users

As you can see from the questionnaire, my users had problems when deleting owners. I have put details of how to deal with this in my user documentation. On the other hand, I found that if I changed the type of relationship between owner and animal tables to allow automatic deletion of animal records, then this problem will not occur, so my users could be worry-free about this problem in future.

Also, my users would like an additional query to print out the number of each type of animal they have on record. They would like to keep details of how these numbers change over the year on a month-by-month basis. I could keep a separate record of these statistics added into a separate table and produce a graph at the end of the year.

Feedback Questionnaire

Please answer the questions in the space allocated and I will collect on the 12th June. Many thanks for your help. David Elliott

1) What did you think of the system overall?
It was generally easy to use but not very professional in the way it looked on the screen

2) Was there any requirement, which was not met?
No on the whole the system seems to meet our requirement

3) Did all the buttons on the screen work properly? Yes/No. Please include details of any which didn't work in the space below.
Yes except for the delete owner. An error message said I could not delete because there was a linked record in the animal table What happens when a pet is due for vaccination?

4) Did the two mail merges work as expected?
Yes but I think the first mail merge letter could be improved. It needs the opening times of the surgery adding so that people ring up when we are open

5) Are the report formats as you expected. Do you need any changes?
Yes they are perfect and for now no changes are necessary

6) Do you feel the system is secure enough for your needs?
Yes we do not need any special security. Just plenty of backups

7) Is the user documentation clear?
Yes it is fine

8) Are there any problems you encountered that you need explaining?
No just the deleting of animal records is an issue

Coursework Adviser's comments

This is an extract showing part of a discussion about the feedback from users. Your questionnaire could again be added into your evaluation, and you can say what improvements are necessary based on what the users say.

- This piece of coursework consists of an assignment that is set by the AQA examination board. It describes a scenario that needs a series of ICT solutions to a number of given tasks.

- In the assignment that follows, you take the role of Frankie Lomax, who is a student at a sixth-form college. As part of your coursework, you have been asked to help Holly Grove High School to improve the organisation of their sports day.

- We will look at **two** tasks from this assignment and use them to show you how to tackle the **Analysis**, **Design**, **Implementation**, **Testing** and **Evaluation** stages. You can then apply the same methods to these stages for all the tasks, in whatever assignment you are set.

- The instructions from the candidate booklet are given in **bold** throughout this section and then explained fully, including extracts from Frankie's coursework.

- Remember that, for the AQA set assignment, all the Analysis for all the tasks must be completed and marked before you move on to the next sections.

⇨ Task 1 (from the candidate's booklet)

Interview between Frankie Lomax and Alison Goldsmith (Head of Girls' PE)

1   **Frankie:** Can you tell me more about the programme? What did you do last year?

2   **Alison:** The programme was a four-page A5 booklet. It was two sheets of A4 that we photocopied back to back and then folded in the middle. The office typed the information. It had a front page with a title. The middle pages contained a list of the events. The back page contained an advert that was stuck on and a typed list of record breakers for last year.

3   **Frankie:** So what do you want this year?

4   **Alison:** Well, what we want is an A5 programme for this year's Sports Day that gives a really good impression of the school. On the first page, we want the school crest (I have this on disk), two photographs of the school (taken with a digital camera), the day and date of the Sports Day and the title 'Sports Day 2002'. What we want you to do is produce two A4 sheets that we can use as masters for the inside and outside of the programme.

5   On the middle pages, we need a list of events as last year, but we need the times added, so competitors know what time to report for their event. I will send these as an e-mail attachment. Naturally, the events should be printed in order of time. We only need to have the track events in the middle pages, because the field events will have already taken place during the morning.

6   For each event, say the 100m, there are eight races. These work out as a boys' race and a girls' race for each year. The exception to this is the 1,500m, which takes place for Year 10 boys only.

7   On the back page, we will have a half-page advert. This year, our sponsor is Helmcroft Hall. They will e-mail their advert to us soon. If you need to change its size, make sure it is kept in the right proportions. We also need to have a list of last year's record breakers on that page. The list of record breakers and the list of the events will need to be in neat columns, with each column having a straight left edge and a bold heading. Each list needs an overall heading. Let's have 'Programme of Events' and 'Records set in 2001'.

8   Now that the school has bought a colour photocopier, we would like to have some colour in the programme.

9   **Frankie:** Where do I find all the information to put in the programme?

10   **Alison:** Well, Sports Day is on Friday, July 12th 2002. The school crest I've got on my computer, so I can either e-mail it to you or give it to you now on a disk. The events and record-breaking lists have yet to be done, and I'll e-mail you that near the time. As soon as we get the advertisement from Helmcroft Hall, I'll forward that to you. I'll use the digital camera to take some photographs around the school and the new school sports hall for the front page and e-mail you these as well.

> ### 1 Read all the material thoroughly.

■ This will help put the assignment into **context** and give an **overview** of the tasks that have to be tackled.

> ### 2 Identify and list the problems the school needs you to solve.

■ It is usually best to carry this out one task at a time, following the instructions given below. Read each task at least twice and **highlight any key points**.

> ### 3 For Task 1, Sports Day Programme, list the following:
> ### a) what form any output will take

■ The **form of the output** will always be given in the candidate's booklet. For Task 1, it is given in paragraph 4:

... produce (print) two A4 sheets (that can be used as masters for the inside and outside of the programme).

> ### b) the information to be output

■ Once the **form** the output will take is clear, decide what **information** will be output, as this will be needed in the Design and Implementation sections. For the Sports Day programme, the information to be output is shown in Figure 3.1.

3.1 *Information to be output*

- On the first page, Alison wants:
  - the school crest and two photographs of the school
  - the day (Friday) and the date (July 12th, 2002)
  - the title 'Sports Day 2002'
    (paragraph 4)

- On the middle pages, Alison wants:
  - a list of events as last year, but with the time added. The events should be printed out in time order. Only the track events are needed.
  - each event has eight races to be output (boys' and girls' races for each year, except the 1,500m, which takes place for Year 10 boys only) (paragraphs 5 and 6)
  This list needs an overall heading 'Programme of Events'
  (paragraph 7)

- On the back page, Alison wants:
  – a half-page advert from the sponsor, Helmcroft Hall
  – a list of last year's record breakers and their events
  This list needs the overall heading 'Records set in 2001'
  (paragraph 7)

c) the data needed to produce the output

■ Now the output has been established, consider what **data** needs to be input to produce that output. It is worth stating where the data to be input will come from (e.g. from disk, e-mail or going to be typed in).

■ There is often an overlap with the section on 'information to output', so think about **cutting and pasting** suitable parts from this section and **adding the data source**. Figure 3.2 shows the sources for the Task 1 output.

3.2 *Sources for Task 1 output*

- On the first page, the following data is needed to produce the output:
  – the school crest (on disk)
  – two photographs of the school (from the digital camera)
  – the day (Friday) and the date (July 12th 2002) (typed in)
  – the title 'Sports Day 2002' (typed in)
     (paragraph 4)

- On the middle pages, the following data is needed to produce output:
  – a list of events as last year, but with time added (e-mail attachment)
  This list needs the overall heading 'Programme of events' – (typed in)
  (paragraphs 5 and 7)

- On the back page, the following data is needed to produce the output:
  – a half-page advert from Helmcroft Hall (to be e-mailed soon)
  – a list of last year's record breakers and their events (e-mail – paragraph 10)
  This list needs the overall heading 'Records set in 2001' (typed in)
  (paragraph 7)

4 For this task, list the performance criteria and desired outcomes.

■ To gain full marks for this section, just list the **performance criteria** and **desired outcomes**. There is no need to explain them.

■ There is often an overlap with the 'information to output' section, so think about **cutting and pasting** suitable parts of this section.

- **Performance criteria** are outcomes that can be 'measured'. **Desired outcomes** are subjective and not as clear cut. The performance criteria and desired outcomes are stated in the candidate booklet, so **do not make up your own**. In your evaluation, you will have to say whether or not these criteria have been met.

- The performance criteria for Task 1 are shown in Figure 3.3.

3.3 Performance criteria for Task 1

- Alison wants an A5 programme. (paragraph 4)
- She wants me to produce two A4 sheets that can be used as masters for the inside and outside of the programme. (end of paragraph 4)
- On the first page Alison wants:
  - the school crest and two photographs of the school
  - the day (Friday) and the date (July 12th 2002)
  - the title 'Sports Day 2002' (paragraph 4)
- On the middle pages, Alison wants:
  - a list of events as last year, but with times added. The events should be printed out in order of time. Only the track events are needed.
  - each event has eight races. These are boys' and girls' races for each year, except the 1,500m which takes place for Year 10 boys only. (paragraphs 5 and 6)

  This list needs the overall heading 'Programme of Events' (paragraph 7)
- On the back page, Alison wants:
  - a half-page advert from the sponsors, Helmcroft Hall. If the size of the advert is changed, it must be kept in the right proportions.
  - a list of last year's record breakers and their events. Each will need to be in neat columns, each column left aligned with a bold heading. (paragraph 7)

  This list needs the overall heading 'Records set in 2001'
- Alison wants some colour in the programme. (paragraph 8)

- For Task1, the only desired outcome is that the programme must give a **really good impression** (paragraph 4).

---

5 For this task, state if testing is needed.

- For this task, no testing is required. If testing is required, the problem will clearly state what testing is needed.

Coursework Adviser's comments
Frankie has produced a **very good, complete analysis** and would be given a mark in the highest mark range (9–10 marks).

⇨ Task 2 (from the candidate's booklet)

Interview with Mary Moneypenny, the School Bursar

1 **Frankie:** Alison Goldsmith asked me to contact you about something called the Holly Grove Price Pledge.

2 **Mary:** Yes, thank you for coming into school. What we want you to do is to produce a model that we can use to predict what is the best price to charge for hot and cold drinks on Sports Day.

3 For Sports Day, the Head teacher has made the Holly Grove Price Pledge to pupils. This is that the school will not make an excessive profit at the Sports Day.

4 The pledge also states that the price of a hot drink will be either 55p or 60p and that the cost of a cold drink will not be more than 60p.

5 The sale of drinks has to cover the cost of the programmes (£175), the hire of the public-address system (£100) and the overtime for the caretaker (£27.50).

6 However, we receive £80 sponsorship from Helmcroft Hall and £50 from the ice-cream van selling sweets and ice cream, but not drinks.

7 The cost to the school to make a hot drink is 15p, and the cost to the school to buy cans of cold drinks is 25p each.

8 **Frankie:** So what number of drinks do you expect to sell?

9 **Mary:** Well, we sell a lot more cold drinks in hot weather. In fact, the Science department have made a study of how many hot and cold drinks were served in the canteen on different days.

10 What they found is on a hot day, 50 hot drinks and 600 cold drinks were sold; on a warm day, 150 hot drinks and 400 cold drinks; on a mild day, 225 hot drinks and 275 cold drinks; on a cool day, 325 hot drinks and 175 cold drinks; on a cold day, 375 hot drinks and 100 cold drinks.

11 For each of the five weather conditions separately, we want you to use the model to show us what to charge for hot and cold drinks so that we make a minimum profit. Of course, we must not make a loss.

12 We know that last year the weather was warm and we sold 150 hot drinks and 400 cold drinks. We know that if we had charged 60p for hot drinks and 54p for cold drinks, then we would have made a £1 profit. If we had charged 53p for cold drinks, then we would have made a loss of £3. Of course, the price of a cold drink has to be a whole number of pence. Can you use this information to test that the model works?

1 For Task 2, Price Pledge Promise Model, list the following:
a) what form any output will take:

■ The form of output for a computer model like this one is usually an interactive **screen display**. Here, variables would be changed, and the results of these changes shown on screen. Produce **printouts** or **screen shots** to show evidence of these screen displays.

■ The output form is a **model** (paragraph 2).

b) the information to be output (remember hard copy output is needed)

■ You need to include precise details of output information in your analysis. In this task, it is the **price** charged for hot and cold drinks, for each of the different weather conditions, that will give the **minimum profit** (paragraph 11). See the Implementation section (pages 117–118) for more details of exactly what output information is expected here.

c) the data needed to produce the output

■ For this task, the data is shown in Figure 3.4.

3.4 *Sources for Task 2 output*

- The costs which need to be typed in (paragraphs 5 and 7):
  - printing programmes   £175
  - public-address system £110
  - caretaker   £27.50
  - cold drink   25p each can
  - hot drink   15p each

- Incomes which again need to be typed in (paragraphs 4 and 6):
  - Helmcroft Hall   £80
  - ice-cream van   £50
  - hot drink   55p or 60p each
  - cold drink   not more than 60p

- Number of drinks sold on days with different types of weather conditions has again got to be typed in (paragraph 10):
  - on a hot day, 50 hot days and 600 cold drinks
  - on a warm day, 150 hot drinks and 400 cold drinks
  - on a mild day, 225 hot drinks and 275 cold drinks
  - on a cool day, 325 hot drinks and 175 cold drinks
  - on a cold day, 375 hot drinks and 100 cold drinks

2 For this task, list the performance criteria and desired outcomes.

■ For Task 2 the **performance criteria** are shown in Figure 3.5.

3.5 *Performance criteria for Task 2*

- The model can be used to predict the best prices to be charged for hot and cold drinks (paragraph 2). In addition, it says, we make a minimum profit. Of course we must not make a loss (paragraph 11).
- The hot drink will cost either 55p or 60p (paragraph 4).
- The cold drink will cost no more than 60p (paragraph 4).
- The sale of drinks has to cover the cost of all the expenditure on Sports Day (paragraph 5).
- The price of a cold drink has to be a whole number of pence (paragraph 12).
- The fixed prices are:
  Costs: printing programmes (£175), hire of public-address system (£110) and overtime for the caretaker (£27.50) (paragraph 5)
  Sponsorship: Helmcroft Hall (£80) and ice-cream van (£50) (paragraph 6).

■ For Task 2, the only desired outcome is that **the school will not make an excessive profit** (paragraph 3).

3 For this task, state if testing is needed.

■ For this task, **testing is required** (paragraph 12).

■ When your analysis for all tasks is complete, your work must be assessed by your teacher. If you have missed any points, your teacher will tell you before you continue with the remainder of your set assignment.

> **Coursework Adviser's comments**
> Frankie has produced a **very good, complete analysis** and would be given a mark in the highest mark range (9–10 marks).

Design a way of solving each problem. This should include: a) a description of how you'll solve the problem, explaining the choices made

- The best way to start this part of the design is to produce some **sketch plans with notes**, outlining what the **final implementation** will look like. Pencil sketches are often the best, as these will stop you going straight onto the computer and starting to implement your solution. **Computer generated sketches are acceptable**, however.

- To illustrate what is needed for this part of the design, we will concentrate on the front and back pages of the School Sports Day programme. You would need to repeat a similar process for the inside pages.

- A good way to start is to produce a **neat sketch** showing layout and details of the content, as shown in Figure 3.6.

3.6 *Layout and content for Task 1*

Back Page   **Front Page**

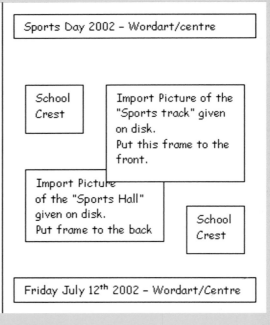

- One way to produce design notes is to **list** them, as shown in Figure 3.7.

Design notes

1 My design is on a piece of A4 landscape paper. The front and back should each be approximately A5.
2 The WordArt that I will use on the front page will be in Arial Black font, light blue in colour and 36pt.
3 Unless my design above says otherwise, I will put all text on the back page into 12pt Times Roman (as it is very clear to read).
4 I will set up tabs to get the list of record breakers, the event and the time/distance into neat columns with a straight left edge.
5 I must make sure the picture of the track goes in front of the picture of the sports hall.
6 I will import pictures, school crest, advert, events and record-breaking lists from disk or e-mail.

Coursework Adviser's comments

This design shows some development. It may be worth Frankie returning to his design plans and modifying them as his implementation progresses.

> **b) the software you will use and the features of the solution that make this software suitable.**

■ Figure 3.8 shows one way of setting out your **description of software usage**.

The software I will use to solve this problem is Microsoft Word. The following table outlines the software features needed to produce the Sports Day Programme, and for each feature, the suitability of Word has been examined.

Feature of the software needed to implement the design	Comment on the suitability of Word to implement this feature
Must be able to position and resize the school crest, pictures of the school, the Helmcroft Hall advert and text boxes.	Word has very good graphic-handling facilities. Text boxes make it fairly simple to import, position and resize graphics. It enables the boxes to be coloured and borders to be added. Word also allows graphics (like the Helmcroft Hall advert) to be kept in the same proportions. These graphic are very easy to import using 'drag and drop'.
Must be able to create bold text for headings and some sub-headings.	Word can make text bold very easily, by simply highlighting the required text and clicking on the 'B' symbol on the formatting toolbar.

- Figure 3.8 gives just two examples of features of software that are needed to implement the design. **You need only refer to features you will actually use.** Some of the other features that need to be described from the original design would be:

  - the need for large, attractive, coloured text on the front page

  - the need for pictures to be placed one in front of another

  - the need to import text and graphics from disk or e-mail

Coursework Adviser's comments

Good Points

- Frankie has developed a planned design and has added some notes to explain the design choices made.
- There is a description of the reasons why the software used is suitable.

Areas for Improvement

- Frankie should try to explain in detail how the design choices made meet the needs of the user.

c) for each problem, design the test plan, if needed

- Testing is not needed for this task, as only judgements on outcomes can be made.

For the Sports Day programme, carefully carry out the solution you have designed.

a) Provide evidence that you have carried it out;

■ This will always require **a final printout or printouts** showing how you have implemented your design (see Figure 3.9).

b) Include enough earlier versions of your work to show the development of your solution and any improvements, corrections or changes from your design

■ This statement implies that **at least two earlier versions** are needed to show development. Figure 3.9 shows only one as an example.

c) add notes to your printouts to make it clear what you done

3.9 *Implementation stages of Task 1*

■ The notes can be **on the printouts themselves** or, as with the design section, they can be presented as a list written **at the end of each early printout**. The notes will say:

• **what** and **how** you have implemented the task so far

• **how** you will proceed with the implementation from this point

• **what changes** you have made from your original design and why you made them.

This is the final printout, showing the implementation of the outside of my Sports Day programme. I was able to follow closely my original design.

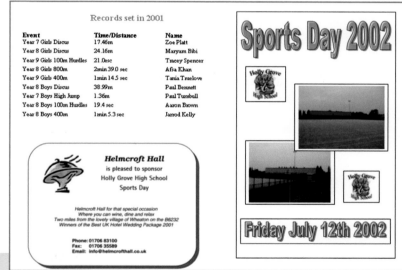

I checked again that everything needed was on the front and the back of the programme.
Some of the stages between the design and the final implementation are shown below.

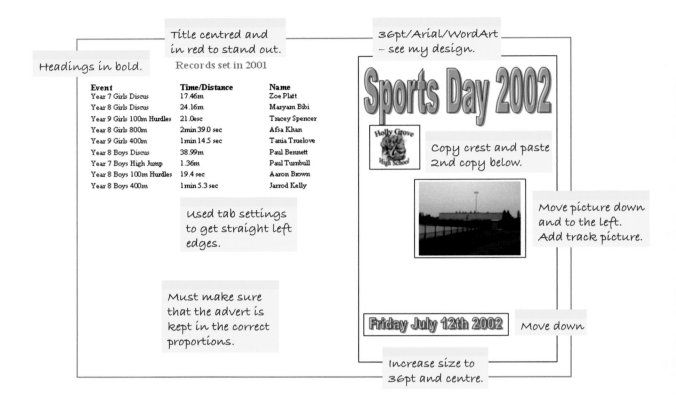

---

d) carry out changes if any tests show they are needed.

■ Even if there are no changes, you should mention this and explain why.

Coursework Adviser's comments

Good Points

- Frankie has produced most of the evidence of the solution, including earlier versions.

Areas for Improvement

- Frankie should use **more notes** to clearly demonstrate his use of **resources** and **techniques** and show a good level of skill, understanding and efficiency.

> **For each problem,**
> a) **review the work you have done and state how successful the solution was**
> b) **discuss how well your solution has met the performance criteria and desired outcomes.**

- **Reviewing** your work and saying how successful your solution was can only be achieved by reference to the **performance criteria** and **desired outcomes**.

- The best way do this is to cut and paste the performance criteria from the Analysis stage into the Evaluation and discuss **how well your solution met these performance criteria**. Your teacher should give you a copy of the complete performance criteria and desired outcomes, in case you missed any.

- Each one should be compared with your solution and you should **comment/discuss** how well each one was met.

- As with the design and implementation sections, the evaluation shown in Figure 3.10 will focus on the front and back pages.

3.10 *Evaluation of Task 1*

- On the first page Alison wants:
  - the school crest and two photographs of the school
  - the day (Friday) and the date (July 12th 2002).
  - the title 'Sports Day 2002' (paragraph 4).

All these have been met by the front page I produced. It contains the school crest, two photos of the school, the day, the date and the title 'Sports Day 2002'. I decided to put on two copies of the school crest; this was partly to fill some 'white space' on the front cover, which improves the impression.

- On the back page Alison wants:
  - a half-page advert from the sponsors, Helmcroft Hall. If the size of the advert is changed, it must be kept in the right proportions (paragraph 7).

The back page I produced contains the half-page advert for the sponsors Helmcroft Hall. I made sure I kept it in the right proportions by dragging at a corner handle on the imported image.

3.10 *continued*

— a list of last year's record breakers and their events. Each will need to be in neat columns, each column left aligned with a bold heading. This list needs the overall heading 'Records set in 2001'

I also fulfilled these success criteria. First, I typed in the overall heading. Then I imported the record breakers and their events from the file given into a text box. I then set up tabs to make sure each column was left aligned, and emboldened the headings. I was pleased that my chosen tab settings kept everything on one line.

- Alison wants some colour in the programme (paragraph 8).

The photographs, the school crest and some of the headings are in colour, so this success criteria was also met. I chose colours which stood out; for example, the red title on the back page made it clear that it was the 'Records set in 2001'.

- Desired outcomes: the programme must give a really good impression (paragraph 4).

The Head of PE said she would be pleased to use a similar programme on our Sports Day. I asked 20 pupils in Year 11 for their opinions of the programme. Eighteen said it gave a really good impression, and only two suggested improvements. Therefore, I think this desired outcome has also been achieved.

Coursework Adviser's comments

Good Points
- Frankie did well to present an evaluation with reasonable reference to the desired outcomes/performance criteria.

Areas for Improvement
- Frankie needs to extend the evaluation and describe the effectiveness of the solution.

Design a way of solving each problem. This should include:
a) a description of how you'll solve the problem, explaining the choices made

- The best way to start this part of the design is to produce some **sketch plans with notes**, outlining what your final implementation will look like. Pencil sketches are often the best, as these will stop you going straight onto the computer and starting to implement your solution.

- Figure 3.11 shows a sample layout with details of content.

3.11 *Sample design layout for Task 2*

	A	B	C	D	E
1	Price Pledge				
2				Cold	Cool
3	Fixed costs - Income			Drinks made	Drinks made
4	Helmcroft Hall sponsorship	80		375	325
5	Ice cream van sponsorship	50		100	175
6	Total fixed costs		Total income		
7					
8	Cost of hot drink - 55p or 60p	0.6			
9	Cost of cold drink - max 60p	0.6			
10				Cold	Cool
11	Fixed costs - expenditure			Drinks made	Drinks made
12	Programme printing	175		375	325
13	Hire of PA system	110		100	175
14	Overtime charges	27.5	Total costs		
15	Total				
16			Profit		
17	Hot drink to buy	0.15			
18	Cold drink to buy	0.25			
19					

Design 1

Here, I've set up a design showing the layout of:

- fixed incomes
- fixed expenditures
- costs of the drinks to buy
- costs of the drinks to sell

My design also shows the layout the model will use to display the various weather conditions. (Here I've only shown the cold and cool conditions, as the rest will follow a similar layout.)

	A	B	C	D	E	F	G	H
1	Price Pledge							
2				Cold	Cool	Mild	Warm	Hot
3	Fixed costs – Income			Drinks made	Drinks made	Drinks made	Drinks made	Drinks made
4	Helmcroft Hall sponsorship	80		375	325	225	150	50
5	Ice cream van sponsorship	50		100	175	275	400	600
6	Total fixed costs	=SUM(B4:B5)	Total income	=D4^B8+D5^B9+B6				
7								
8	Cost of hot drink – 55p or 60p	0.6						
9	Cost of cold drink – max 60p	0.6						
10				Cold	Cool	Mild	Warm	Hot
11	Fixed costs – expenditure			Drinks made	Drinks made	Drinks made	Drinks made	Drinks made
12	Programme printing	175		375	325	225	150	50
13	Hire of PA system	110		100	175	275	400	600
14	Overtime charges	27.5	Total costs	=D12^B17+D13^B18+B15				
15	Total	=SUM(B12:B14)						
16			Profit	=D6-D14				
17	Hot drink to buy	0.15						
18	Cold drink to buy	0.25						
19								

3.11 *continued*

Design 2

Next the formulae to be used need to be considered.

- I produced these pencil designs on a spreadsheet layout plan that was provided by the teacher.
- I will use Times Roman 12pt font unless I say otherwise.
- I will vary the column widths manually to fit the contents, but columns D to H will be kept the same width to help improve my presentation.
- I will keep the formulae I use simple, only using addition and multiplication.

b) the software you will use and the features of the solution that make this software suitable

- If there is more than one obvious choice of software for the task, you should mention **both options** and then **explain your choice**, referring to both **advantages** and **disadvantages**.

The software I will use to solve this problem is Microsoft Excel. The following table outlines the software features needed to produce my Price Pledge Model, and for each feature, the suitability of Excel has been examined.

Feature needed to implement the design	Comment on the suitable of Excel to implement this feature
If I am to use the software efficiently, it must be capable of copying (replicating) formulae down or to the right.	Excel has a simple-to-use replicate feature. I can select a cell (that contains a text, number or a formulae), highlight a section to the right and copy the contents of the original cell into those selected to the right. It will automatically change the letter for the column being used as it's replicated across.
I need the software to be able to carry out simple calculations.	Excel can carry out simple calculations. For example, I need it to calculate the cost of hot drinks, e.g. D4*B8.

3.12 *Software used for Task 2*

- Only two features have been looked at here. **Other features would need to be considered.**

Coursework Adviser's comments

Good Points
- Frankie has developed a planned design and has added some notes to explain the design choices made. He has also indicated the formulae he would use.
- There is a description of the reasons why the software used is suitable.

Areas for Improvement
- Frankie should try to explain in detail how the design choices made meet the needs of the user.

c) for each problem, design the test plan, if needed

■ Testing is needed for this task, so a test plan is required (see Figure 3.13).

3.13 *Test plan for Task 2*

Test Plan

Test Data
This data is given from last year:
On a warm day, 150 hot drinks and 400 cold drinks were sold.
Cost of drinks: 60p for hot drinks and 54p charged for cold drinks gives a £1 profit.
Cost of drinks: 60p for hot drinks and 53p charged for cold drinks gives a £3 loss.

Manual Check – all the fixed data will be typed into the model

Fixed Income		Fixed Expenditure	
Helmcroft Hall	£80	Programme printing	£175
Ice-cream van	£50	Hire of public-address	£110
Total	£130	Overtime – caretaker	£27.50
Total			£312.50

Warm day – drinks sold
Number of hot drinks　　= 150　　Hot drink to buy: 15p
Number of cold drinks　　= 400　　Cold drink to buy: 25p

Test 1
I will input the costs for the hot and cold drinks given below into the model. I will compare the actual results with the expected ones. I may make modifications if the two results do not match.
Cost of hot drink: 60p
Cost of cold drink: 54p

Profit = income – expenditure
= (130 + (150×60) + (400×54)) – (312.5 + (150×15) + (400×25))
= £436 – £435
= £1 profit
This agrees with the figure given in the booklet.

Test 2 – as for Test 1, but with the cost of cold drinks being reduced to 53p
Cost of hot drink: 60p
Cost of cold drink: 53p
Profit = (130 + (150×60) + (400×53)) – (312.5 + 150×15) + (400×25))
= £432 – £435
= £3 loss
This agrees with the figure give in the booklet.

Coursework Adviser's comments
See comments on page 126.

For the **Price Pledge Model**, carefully carry out the solution you have designed.

- Add **notes** to your to your printouts to make it clear what you have done, as shown in Figures 3.14 and 3.15.

- Provide **evidence** that you have carried out the task. In the case of a model, a printout of the formulae is always needed (see Figure 3.15).

- Include **earlier versions** of your work to show development.

3.14 Printouts showing development

Printout 1

	A	B	C	D	E	F	G	H
1	Price Pledge							
2				Cold	Cool	Mild	Warm	Hot
3	Fixed costs - Income			Drinks made	Drinks made	Drinks made	Drinks made	Drinks made
4	Helmcroft Hall sponsorship	80		375	325	225	150	50
5	Ice cream van sponsorship	50		100	175	275	400	600
6	Total fixed costs		Total Income					
7								
8	Cost of hot drink - 55p or 60p	0.6						
9	Cost of cold drink - max 60p	0.6						
10				Cold	Cool	Mild	Warm	Hot
11	Fixed costs - expenditure			Drinks made	Drinks made	Drinks made	Drinks made	Drinks made
12	Programme printing	175		375	325	225	150	50
13	Hire of PA system	110		100	175	275	400	600
14	Overtime charges	27.5	Total costs					
15	Total							
16			Profit					
17	Hot drink to buy	0.15						
18	Cold drink to buy	0.25						
19								

This is the layout of my model as I set it up from my Design 1.
I have entered the incomes and expenditures given into the model.
I have not entered any formulae at this stage.
I have taken care to keep the text and the numbers in the same cells as in my design.

Printout 2

	A	B	C	D	E	F	G	H
1	Price Pledge							
2				Cold	Cool	Mild	Warm	Hot
3	Fixed costs - Income			Drinks made	Drinks made	Drinks made	Drinks made	Drinks made
4	Helmcroft Hall sponsorship	£80.00		£375.00	£325.00	£225.00	£150.00	£50.00
5	Ice cream van sponsorship	£50.00		£100.00	£175.00	£275.00	£400.00	£600.00
6	Total fixed costs	£130.00	Total Income	£415.00	£430.00	£430.00	£460.00	£520.00
7								
8	Cost of hot drink - 55p or 60p	£0.60						
9	Cost of cold drink - max 60p	£0.60						
10				Cold	Cool	Mild	Warm	Hot
11	Fixed costs - expenditure			Drinks made	Drinks made	Drinks made	Drinks made	Drinks made
12	Programme printing	£175.00		£375.00	£325.00	£225.00	£150.00	£50.00
13	Hire of PA system	£110.00		£100.00	£175.00	£275.00	£400.00	£600.00
14	Overtime charges	£27.50	Total costs	£393.75	£405.00	£415.00	£435.00	£470.00
15	Total	£312.50						
16			Profit	£21.25	£25.00	£15.00	£25.00	£50.00
17	Hot drink to buy	£0.15						
18	Cold drink to buy	£0.25						
19								

I have put in the formulae to calculate totals.
I have started with a maximum price of 60p for hot and 60p for cold drinks.
This shows the profit made on a warm day.

	A	B	C	D	E	F	G	H
1	Price Pledge							
2				Cold	Cool	Mild	Warm	Hot
3	Fixed costs - Income			Drinks made	Drinks made	Drinks made	Drinks made	Drinks made
4	Helmcroft Hall sponsorship	80		375	325	225	150	50
5	Ice cream van sponsorship	50		100	175	275	400	600
6	Total fixed costs	=SUM(B4:B5)	Total Income	=D4'B8+D5'B9+B6	=E4'B8+E5'B9+B6	=F4'B8+F5'B9+B6	=G4'B8+G5'B9+B6	=H4'B8+H5'B9+B6
7								
8	Cost of hot drink - 55p or 60p	0.6						
9	Cost of cold drink - max 60p	0.6						
10				Cold	Cool	Mild	Warm	Hot
11	Fixed costs - expenditure			Drinks made	Drinks made	Drinks made	Drinks made	Drinks made
12	Programme printing	175		375	325	225	150	50
13	Hire of PA system	110		100	175	275	400	600
14	Overtime charges	27.5	Total costs	=D12'B17+D13'B18+B15	=E12'B17+E13'B18+B15	=F12'B17+F13'B18+B15	=G12'B17+G13'B18+B15	=H12'B17+H13'B18+B15
15	Total	=SUM(B12:B14)						
16			Profit	=D6-D14	=E6-E14	=F6-F14	=G6-G14	=H6-H14
17	Hot drink to buy	0.15						
18	Cold drink to buy	0.25						
19								
20								

3.15 *Printout showing formulae*

Printout 3
Here are the formulae I used.

Coursework Adviser's comments

Good Points
- Frankie has produced most of the evidence of the solution, including earlier versions, and has provided a printout of the formulae used.
- He has included some notes to show that resources have been used with some skill and understanding.

Areas for Improvement
- Frankie could have used more notes to clearly demonstrate his use of resources and techniques and to show a good level of skill, understanding and efficiency.

a) carry out the test plan

■ Figure 3.16 shows how the spreadsheet formulae can be tested.

3.16 Test plan for Task 2

Test 1 – using the Test Data

150 hot drinks at 60p   400 cold drinks at 54p   Weather conditions: warm

	A	B	C	D	E	F	G	H
1	Price Pledge							
2				Cold	Cool	Mild	Warm	Hot
3	Fixed costs - Income			Drinks made	Drinks made	Drinks made	Drinks made	Drinks made
4	Helmcroft Hall sponsorship	£80.00		375	325	225	150	50
5	Ice cream van sponsorship	£50.00		100	175	275	400	600
6	Total fixed costs	£130.00	Total Income	£409.00	£419.50	£413.50	£436.00	£484.00
7								
8	Cost of hot drink - 55p or 60p	£0.60						
9	Cost of cold drink - max 60p	£0.54						
10				Cold	Cool	Mild	Warm	Hot
11	Fixed costs - expenditure			Drinks made	Drinks made	Drinks made	Drinks made	Drinks made
12	Programme printing	£175.00		375	325	225	150	50
13	Hire of PA system	£110.00		100	175	275	400	600
14	Overtime charges	£27.50	Total costs	£393.75	£405.00	£415.00	£435.00	£470.00
15	Total	£312.50						
16			Profit	£15.25	£14.50	-£1.50	£1.00	£14.00
17	Hot drink to buy	£0.15						
18	Cold drink to buy	£0.25						
19								

3.15 Printouts showing development

Expected results
I expect the profit for this test data to be £1. This is shown in my Test Plan.

Comparison
The actual result was £1. As this agrees with my expected result, Test 1 has been successful.

Test 2 – using the Test Data
150 hot drinks at 60p   400 cold drinks at 53p   Weather conditions: warm

	A	B	C	D	E	F	G	H
1	Price Pledge							
2				Cold	Cool	Mild	Warm	Hot
3	Fixed costs - Income			Drinks made	Drinks made	Drinks made	Drinks made	Drinks made
4	Helmcroft Hall sponsorship	£80.00		375	325	225	150	50
5	Ice cream van sponsorship	£50.00		100	175	275	400	600
6	Total fixed costs	£130.00	Total Income	£408.00	£417.75	£410.75	£432.00	£478.00
7								
8	Cost of hot drink - 55p or 60p	£0.60						
9	Cost of cold drink - max 60p	£0.53						
10				Cold	Cool	Mild	Warm	Hot
11	Fixed costs - expenditure			Drinks made	Drinks made	Drinks made	Drinks made	Drinks made
12	Programme printing	£175.00		375	325	225	150	50
13	Hire of PA system	£110.00		100	175	275	400	600
14	Overtime charges	£27.50	Total costs	£393.75	£405.00	£415.00	£435.00	£470.00
15	Total	£312.50						
16			Profit	£14.25	£12.75	-£4.25	-£3.00	£8.00
17	Hot drink to buy	£0.15						
18	Cold drink to buy	£0.25						
19								

Expected results
I expect the loss for this test data to be £3 (i.e. –£3). This is shown in my Test Plan..

Comparison
The actual result was –£3. As this agrees with my expected result, Test 2 has been successful.

3.16 *continued*

Coursework Adviser's comments

Good Points
- Frankie has produced a detailed test plan and has identified all the data to be used to check the problem.
- Testing against the test plan has been carried out, and a record of results has been produced.

Areas for Improvement
- Frankie needs to describe any changes needed as a result of testing.

> **Review the work done and discuss how well your solution has met the performance criteria and desired outcomes.**

■ Cut and paste the **performance criteria** from the Analysis stage and discuss how well the solution met each of these performance criteria, as shown in Figure 3.17.

3.17 *Evaluation of Task 2*

● Produce a model that can be used to predict the best prices to be charged for hot and cold drinks (paragraph 2). In addition, make minimum profit, without making a loss (paragraph 11).

The testing I carried out earlier shows that I can use my model to predict the best prices to be charged for hot and cold drinks. Both Test 1 and Test 2 show this. In addition, they also show that a minimum profit was made without making a loss.

● The hot drink will cost either 55p or 60p (paragraph 4).
  The cold drink will cost no more than 60p (paragraph 4).

Both of the conditions were met. This again can be seen from my testing section. My model was set up so that the cost of a hot drink must be chosen from a list that only contains 55p or 60p. Next to the cell where the cost of the cold drink is to be typed in is a reminder that the maximum cost must be 60p.

● The sale of drinks has to cover the cost involved in Sports Day (paragraph 5).

This really means the same thing as the success criteria given above which says 'Of course, we must not make a loss'. So again, Test 1 and Test 2 both show that no loss was made.

● The price of a cold drink has to be a whole number of pence (paragraph 12).

I set the price field for cold drinks to be currency displaying two decimal places. This means it is only possible for the price of cold drinks to be entered in whole number of pence.

● The fixed prices are:
  Costs – printing programmes (£175), hire of public-address system (£110) and overtime for the caretaker (£27.50) (paragraph 5)
  Sponsorship – Helmcroft Hall (£80) and ice-cream van (£50) (paragraph 6)

All these fixed prices were all typed into my model and checked. Printouts of both the implementation and the testing show that these figures have been input correctly.

Coursework Adviser's comments

Good Points
● Frankie did well to present an **evaluation** with **reasonable reference** to the desired outcomes/performance criteria.

Areas for Improvement
● Frankie needs to extend the evaluation and describe the **effectiveness** of the solution.

⇨ Guidance on suitable projects

■ Choose a topic that interests you! You will spend a number of weeks working on your project, so it should motivate and involve you. Your teacher will advise you about suitability.

■ Choose something that has the right scope for a project – **think small!**

■ The best projects are generated by **genuine user needs**; for example, running a small business provides a good range of potential ICT activities:
  • How can the business generate more customers?
    (e.g. need to improve advertising)
  • How can the manager check what stock is available?
    (e.g. need quicker ways of locating stock and knowing its availability)
  • What can the manager do in the case of staff absence?
    (e.g. need a system with immediate access to employees' details)
  • How can the manager respond if the bank manager wishes to check up on the business plan?
    (e.g. need a regular way of checking on profitability).

■ Other types of activities which lend themselves to a project are:
  • Organising an event, such as a school activity day (e.g. ten-pin bowling or Geography field trip).
  • Collecting information for a specific purpose, e.g. by conducting a questionnaire ('Why aren't school meals more popular?').

■ Here are lists of projects which have previously worked well:

Small business	Organising an event	Collecting information for a purpose
Restaurant	School sports team	School meals
Newsagent's	Annual ski trip	Smoking
Computer shop	A foreign-exchange visit	Music tastes
Doctor's surgery	School tuck shop	School uniform
Estate agent	Year 11 leavers' ball	Health

HINTS

• Think small (e.g. a corner shop) – don't be overambitious.

• Ensure the background is clear.

• In general, consider between three and five sub-problems, which should be linked.

• Remember, it isn't just the number of sub-problems that you tackle, it is the effectiveness of the way that you tackle them that matters.

■ Projects such as these should provide **between three and five suitable sub-problems** for you to tackle during your ICT coursework. Sometimes one complex sub-problem, such as a bookings system, would be enough. Try not to do more than five sub-problems. If you identify more sub-problems than this, then prioritise.

■ Make sure that the sub-problems are **sufficiently different** from each other. This will allow you to show a range of techniques. The sub-problems should be linked together.

■ After you have done the analysis, you have to **design, implement, test** and **evaluate** your solution and produce a **user guide** for reusable sections. All of these depend on how effective your analysis is.

■ The examples that follow focus on running a small business – the same principles apply to other types of project activities.

UNIT 1: ANALYSIS

  Overview: How to begin research

Overview

- Items you need to include in your analysis are summarised in the table below. They are then explained in more detail, with extracts from a student's work, in the rest of this section.

- Analysis is one of the sections of the project where your **spelling, punctuation** and **grammar** will be judged. Your **presentation** and **use of a range of specialist terms** will also be taken into account.

> **MARK ALLOCATION**
>
> Analysis is the first stage of the project for AQA GCSE specification A. The maximum mark you can be awarded for analysis is 15.

Items to include	Advice
Research	Find out some facts about the problem. This is not part of the formal assessment, but it is helpful to provide background data.
Introduction	Provide a scenario by writing about the background and emphasising the problems from the user's viewpoint (Figure 4.2).
List three to five sub-problems	A few sub-problems which require different types of techniques to solve are needed (Figure 4.3). The exception is one complex sub-problem, such as a bookings system.
Evaluate ways of tackling the sub-problems	Think of at least two **different** ways of tackling each problem, e.g. a manual way compared with a computer technique (Figures 4.4 and 4.5).
Show the form of output	Indicate how the solution will look (e.g. printout, on screen) when it's produced (Figure 4.6).
Show the information to be output	Describe what information has to be in the solution (Figure 4.6).
Consider the data needed to produce the output	What data is needed to solve the sub-problem (Figure 4.6).
Recognise ways in which the solutions may be reusable over time	If the solution is to be reusable, think about how the data may change over a period of days or weeks (Figure 4.6).
Describe the links between the sub-problems	To achieve higher marks, think about the whole solution and consider ways in which sub-problems are linked together – they may, for example, use common data (Figure 4.7).
Specify the desired outcomes and performance criteria to be used in evaluating the solution	For your solution to be successful, you need to specify the criteria against which you will judge it (Figures 4.8 and 4.9).

- There are some significant differences between the project and the assignment. In the project:

  - you must **describe** and **explain** all the information, not just list it

  - you are expected to make sure that some solutions to the sub-problems are **reusable**

  - you must show how some sub-problems link together.

- In this and the following units, we will be using extracts from Rachel's project on a computer shop to explain what coursework advisers look for in the analysis stage of the project. The context for your project will be different, but the stages you need to work through will be the same.

⇨ How to begin

- When you begin your project, you will not always know what information is needed, if it is relevant or even how much to include. **Word-process your ideas**, so that if changes are needed, it is easier to update. You can also cut and paste incorrectly placed sections where they should go. Your finished analysis should be several pages long. A well-researched and thought-out analysis affects the rest of your project.

- A basic **spider diagram** to show your initial thoughts about sub-problems and links between them is a good idea. Rachel's is shown in Figure 4.1.

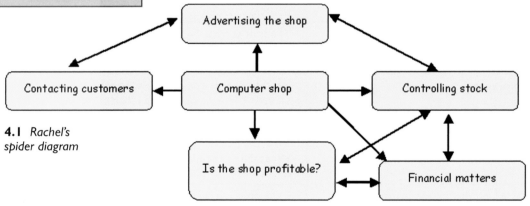

4.1 Rachel's spider diagram

⇨ Researching your analysis

- Think about the **reasons** for choosing your project and some **questions** to which you need to know the answer. You can then research them to provide the background.

- If your project is about running a small business, plan to **visit** the company to find out more about it. **Write a letter** to the company explaining what you are doing and what help you require.

- Talk to family and friends who may be able to help. Perhaps **produce a simple questionnaire** or a **set of interview questions**. This will help in the fact-finding stage of your analysis.

■ The background to your project should provide information about activities which aren't currently working well. These become your **sub-problems**, which you will later use ICT techniques to solve.

4.2 Extract from Rachel's introduction

<u>Research</u>

I plan to investigate the running of the computer shop **'Bytes for all'**. I regularly visit it to buy computer components and media. Because of this, I already know some of its background. I plan to interview the owner to get her views and take some notes when I am next there.

<u>Background</u>

The computer shop ('Bytes for all') is situated in a side street off the High Street in Derwen. The shop sells the usual range of computers, laptops, printers, computer components, media, printer paper and cartridges. On Saturday afternoons, when high-street shops seem to be full of potential customers, there are only a few regular customers in 'Bytes for all'. Ms Byte (the owner) wonders why this happens.

Ms Byte has now realised that once a customer buys from a shop, they may use that same shop time and time again. How can she make customers more aware of the shop and its stock? How will they associate the shop with its adverts?

Some customers live a long distance away from 'Bytes for all'. Ms Byte hasn't the time to be able to respond to their telephone requests about what new stock is in store before they travel a long distance to see it. How can she respond to this?

If customers come into the shop and ask for something unusual, Ms Byte never knows whether she has it in stock. If she hasn't got the item, she doesn't immediately know who to order it from. Also she would like to reduce the amount of time she spends checking and ordering stock. What can she do about this?

Another time-consuming aspect of the business is checking up on the money coming in and going out of the business. Ms Byte never knows whether she is making a profit or not. To keep her bank manager happy, how can she sort this out without using up valuable time spent with customers?

Coursework Adviser's comments

Good Points
- Rachel's background provides a 'reasonable description' of the problems faced by the shop (i.e. it would allow her to achieve high marks for this aspect).

Areas for Improvement
- There is little evidence of any direct research which would give the problems more relevance.
- More time should be spent explaining how the problems interfere with the running of the business.
- The background lacks some clarity and detail.
- At this stage, there are no obvious relationships identified between the problems.

Identifying and analysing sub-problems

HINTS

- If you describe the background in sufficient detail, the sub-problems will emerge from this.
- Make a list of your sub-problems. Then analyse each one in further detail.

- In Rachel's project, **publishing**, in all its forms, is a sub-problem. For example, if advertising is needed to increase the number of customers, then there are various forms it could take: catchy shop name, logo, poster, leaflet, flier, brochure, business card, headed paper, newspaper advert, web-based advertising or e-mails to customers.

- Some of these, such as a poster or monthly leaflet, are potentially reusable (meaning they can be redone several times for different effects), whereas others aren't (e.g. a logo or business card).

- A poster could be set up and saved as a **master form** or **template**. This could be used for all future posters. Much of the basic information will remain the same, but some (e.g. new stock or special offers) will change regularly.

- A further sub-problem might be how to allow current customers to see, from their own home, what new stock is in store. **Web page(s)** or **e-mail newsletter(s)** would be appropriate. Both web pages and e-mail newsletters are potentially reusable.

HINTS

- Remember, a lot of trivial sub-problems won't make a good project, whereas a few substantial ones will.
- List between three and five sub-problems which show some links between them.

4.3 *Extract from Rachel's list of sub-problems*

List of sub-problems

1. a) • How can I advertise **'Bytes for all'** to increase the number of customers?
   - What type of advertising is best for the shop?
   - Will the adverts link together?
   b) • From their home, how can I enable customers to see what new stock is in store?
   - What is the best electronic method of doing this for customers who live a long way from 'Bytes for all'?
2. • How can Ms Byte organise her stock so that she can find what types of stock she has in?
   - Can a system be set up to make it easy to re-order from her suppliers?
3. What is a quick way of letting Ms Byte know whether she is making a profit or not?

Coursework Adviser's comments

Good Points

- Rachel has stated the sub-problems which are necessary for this aspect.
- There is a **sufficient number** of suitable sub-problems for a substantial project.

Areas for Improvement

- A **clearer description** about how the sub-problems affect the running of the business would have scored more highly.

- One possible way of tackling the publishing sub-problem is a poster. It could be produced manually using paper and writing implements (e.g. pen, paintbrush), although in some circumstances a manual method may be inappropriate. Remember to consider **ICT techniques** (software such as a presentation package, a graphics package or a desktop-publishing package). Consider the **advantages** and **disadvantages** of each method.

- If handling data records is a sub-problem, a manual solution may be using a card-index system. The ICT technique to compare with could be using software such as a database.

- If calculating profit is sub-problem, a manual method may be using a calculator and paper. An alternative ICT technique could involve using software such as a spreadsheet.

> **HINT**
> For each sub-problem, remember to consider the advantages and disadavantages of each approach.

4.4 *Extract from Rachel's ways of tackling sub-problems*

Ways of tackling the advertising problem

To enable Ms Byte to attract more customers, she has to be able to advertise more effectively. Ms Byte is going to concentrate on this by using posters which will be displayed in the High Street. The posters will include a logo which will also be displayed inside the shop. This will allow 'Bytes for all' advertising to be closely linked with the shop.

Poster
I could produce the poster by a manual method such as using paper and paint.
Manual method – Advantages: Doing it manually would be easy, as I don't have to learn particular skills. If I were a good artist, then it would be effective. I would have the paint and paper readily available. It would be cheap to produce because there are only minimal costs – such as paper and paint. This idea would work for a special 'one-off' poster if I had artistic talent.
Manual method – Disadvantages: If I made a mistake, I would have to re-start, which would slow me down. Every colour copy would have to be produced individually, which would take a long time for several copies. A big disadvantage would be if I weren't very good at art, as the finished poster wouldn't be attractive to customers.

An alternative way of doing it would be to use software such as Publisher.
Computer technique – Advantages: With Publisher, I could use a large range of colours for the text, background and special effects. The software would allow me to save my work and continue it when convenient. Any mistakes that I make are easily changed, and if my plan turned out to be inaccurate, it is easy to amend. Images and pictures could be imported into the poster without needing artistic talent to do them. I could print the exact number of copies that I need. Also, if I set up a template for my poster, it could be reusable. When I return to it next time, I could add further news or information for my customers.
Computer technique – Disadvantages: I would need to learn how to use the features of the software to produce the poster. The software costs money to buy, and you need to have a computer and printer to use it.

■ Figure 4.5 shows some outlines of different ways to tackle the other sub-problems.

4.5 *Extract from Rachel's ways of tackling other sub-problems*

The next step as part of the publishing sub-problem would be to look at alternative ways of enabling customers to see what new stock is in store. The fact that they live a long distance from the shop is a further problem.

The alternatives that Ms Byte could consider would be electronic ones, as the post is too slow for this purpose.

- Perhaps she could send out an e-mail bulletin to all her customers. Some may consider this an infringement of their privacy (spam) and want a method where they decide when they want to view new stock.
- She could prepare a website which will also use the shop logo. It would have page(s) showing new stock which had just arrived. This would mean that the page(s) would have to be updated regularly – perhaps each week would be sufficient.

In addition Ms Byte needs to consider ways of organising her stock.

The ways that Ms Byte might consider are:

- Having a card-index system with each item of stock named. Each card would need to contain the price paid, the quantity in stock, which shelf it was kept on, the supplier's details and when it was ordered.
- Using one database for the stock details and one for the supplier details.
- Setting up a database, containing separate tables for the stock and suppliers. The tables would need to be linked so that orders could be placed for the correct items and sent to the correct address. This would reduce data duplication and data-entry errors.

Ms Byte has a third sub-problem to analyse – how will she know whether she is making a profit?

The alternatives that Ms Byte could think about are:

- She could use pencil and paper with an accounting book to record all the payments she makes and all the income she receives each day. Then work out the results using a calculator to find the profit.
- She could set up a system which automatically calculates the total sales and payments for each day. Each week, it would calculate the total profit made. The weekly balance and any fixed payments could automatically be transferred to the start of the following week. The system could accept data transferred from the stock database table to reduce data-entry errors and establish links between two parts of the system.

Coursework Adviser's comments

Good Points

- Rachel has **identified and evaluated** more than one way of tackling these sub-problems, which will allow her to achieve a high mark for this aspect.
- The ways of tackling the sub-problems are all **relevant**.

Areas for Improvement

- Rachel should **identify which method is best** and state it.

■ Think about the **outcomes,** not only for the final solution, but also as an aid when you start on the design. The four main areas to consider are the **form** and the **information** to output the **data** needed to produce it and ways in which the solution may be **reusable.** Figure 4.6 shows Rachel's summary of outcomes for her computer-shop poster.

HINT
Consider what your solutions will need to look like (the outcomes).

⇨ The form of the output

■ The **outcome** is what the finished solution will look like when you have completed it. So you must include the form of the output – what it will look like, what size it is and how it will be set out.

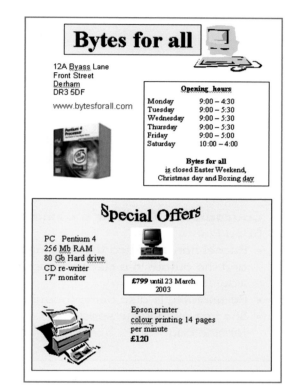

⇨ The information to output

■ Specify the **information to output,** for example 'that a poster contains the shop's name and logo, its location and opening times'. Other information that could be output on a poster is the new stock arriving.

⇨ Data needed to produce the output

■ Think about the **data needed to produce the output.** If possible, avoid using real names, addresses and telephone numbers, as there may be confidentiality issues. The data you need will be typical data, which includes text, numbers and images.

⇨ Recognising ways in which the solutions may be reusable over time

■ Any regular changes to a poster which make it **reusable,** such as this month's special offers, should be identified.

HINT
Think about what data is needed to produce your solutions.

4.6 *Extract from Rachel's outcomes*

Computer shop poster

<u>Outcomes</u>

<u>Form of output:</u> The poster will be in A4 portrait orientation, with the top two-thirds showing fixed information. The bottom third will include a frame for special offers.

<u>Information to output:</u> The poster will have the shop name ('Bytes for all') near the top of the page and the logo above it. The shop's address will appear immediately underneath. Below that will be the opening times. This information will be the same for all my posters.

<u>Reusable data:</u> The bottom third of the poster will contain details about new stock and special offers. This information will change regularly when I print a new poster.

<u>Data needed:</u> The data that will remain the same is the shop's name, logo and address. For the reusable data, (e.g. special offers), I could use Internet computer sites to provide me with up-to-date information about specifications and prices of computer items.

Coursework Adviser's comments

Good Points

- Rachel has specified the data needed and the output in a clear and appropriate way.
- Re-usability is also being thought about.
- She has used some specialist terminology.

Areas for Improvement

- Rachel should state why she has chosen to split the fixed and reusable information in this way.

- The spider diagram (see Figure 4.1 on page 132) is a useful starting point for **relationships** as it shows the outline links.

- Relationships show the way in which parts of the sub-problems are linked together. The link can be simple, e.g. the same data is imported into different parts of the solution, or it may be more complex, e.g. the results of one part of the solution may influence another part. **Data links** are the most obvious way of showing relationship between the sub-problems.

4.7 *Extract from Rachel's relationships*

Relationships

Computer-shop logo

A way in which I could link my adverts together is if I include the same logo in each advert. The logo should be easily identifiable as belonging to the shop. I will import the logo into some of the adverts. I will make it larger when I use it in the poster and place it centrally above the shop's name. I will resize it to a smaller size to appear on each page of the website.

Stock database

I will link the stock database table to the supplier's database table. This is so that I can produce reports and order what I need from the correct company, without having to type it out again.

Re-ordering extra stock

I will use the supplier's database table to mail-merge letters, re-ordering extra stock from them on specified dates.

Receipts and payments system

I will export part of the data from the stock database into the spreadsheet of receipts and payments to calculate the monthly profit.

Coursework Adviser's comments

Good Points
- The **spider diagram** (Figure 4.1) has provided a useful starting point for the relationships.
- Rachel has shown a good understanding of the **relationships** that are needed between various sub-problems. Her overall mark would be towards the highest mark range for those problems considered.

Areas for Improvement
- Rachel should describe more clearly the exact nature of the links between the sub-problems. She should specify how the two tables will be linked and what fields from the supplier's table will be used for the mail-merge letters.

Specifying desired outcomes and performance criteria

- Having analysed each sub–problem, considered alternative ways of tackling them and decided on the data needed and the outcomes, the next step is to set out **criteria** against which you will **judge** your solution.

- If your solution matches your criteria, you will have been successful.

- Performance criteria are **conditions** which you expect your solution to be able to meet. This is an important element, as it affects your ability to evaluate your solution at the end.

4.8 *Extract from Rachel's summary of performance criteria*

Performance criteria and desired outcomes

Computer-shop poster

The poster will contain **all required details**. It will be printed in **colour** on **A4** paper in **portrait**. The top two-thirds of the poster will always be the same. The bottom third will change.

The poster will be **reusable** because a template of the fixed items on the poster will be saved with an empty frame in the bottom third. It will be saved as **Poster template**.

- Figure 4.9 shows some of the **possible desired outcomes** and **performance criteria** for the other sub-problems.

4.9 *Extract from Rachel's summary of other performance criteria*

Website

- Total of four pages
- Consistent layout and style
- Shop name and logo on each page
- Hyperlinks from home page to each other page
- A page with computers for sale
- A page with computer peripherals for sale
- A page with new stock, which will be updated regularly
- A hyperlink from each page back to the home page, using the logo or a text message

Stock relational database

- A stock table with essential details (ID, type, description, date, cost and selling price, re-order level, amount ordered, quantity and supplier code)
- A supplier table with essential details (supplier code, name, address, postcode)
- A way of showing stock of a certain type
- A way of showing under-stocked items
- A way of linking the tables so that orders could be placed for the correct items and sent to the correct supplier.
- A way of re-ordering under-stocked items

Profit/loss system
- The system automatically calculates the total sales and payments for each day.
- The system automatically calculates the total weekly profit made.
- The profit stands out.
- The weekly balance and any fixed payments are automatically transferred to the start of the following week.
- The system accepts data transferred from the stock database table.
- The system is quick and easy to use.

Coursework Adviser's comments

Good Points
- Rachel has identified performance criteria against which the solution can be measured – again, high quality for this aspect.
- Reusability has been thought about.

Areas for Improvement
- Rachel should describe the performance criteria for *each sub-problem*, which she can then paste into the Evaluation section of her project as a starting point.
- The 'required details' in the poster are insufficiently explained and need clarifying.

UNIT 2: DESIGN

◼ Designing for publishing sub-problems ◼

MARK ALLOCATION

The maximum mark you can be awarded for Design is 20. There are many aspects to Design. This unit has been split into three sessions to show you what is required for a good design.

HINTS

- A good design would allow someone else to produce your solution, exactly as you wanted.
- Publishing should be considered as one sub-problem – don't try too many sub-tasks.
- When your design is complete, it should have a plan and a justification for choosing the software.
- Although all the design has to be presented together, it is more efficient to produce, test and evaluate sub-problems as you go along, before proceeding to design the next sub-problem.

⇨ **Information required for the publishing section**

- List the information required for each of the published documents (e.g. logo, poster, headed paper, flier, business card, website, etc.) that you have identified as needed to solve the problem – **don't choose too many**. For each document there will be some information which is not reusable.

⇨ **Logo**

- A **logo** shows an 'image' of the business. It may incorporate the business name. The logo should be **resizeable** so that it can be used in different parts of the publishing solution.

⇨ **Poster**

- Some information required on a poster will be **fixed**. However, things such as special offers will change regularly. The fixed information on a poster can be saved as a template and reused regularly to show different special offers. A logo can be imported and resized to fit.

Information required for my poster

The fixed information on my poster will be the shop's name, logo, address, website and opening times. The reusable data will be in a frame in the bottom third of the poster – it will contain the special offers that 'Bytes for all' makes regularly.

4.10 *Extract from Rachel's information for the poster*

⇨ **Headed paper**

- Headed paper is only produced once. Information has to be presented in an **attractive format** on a **specific paper size**.

Information required for my letter-headed paper

The fixed information needs to contain the business name, address, logo, telephone number, fax, e-mail address and website. The letter-headed paper is not reusable, but I may use the finished version to link parts of the solution – for example, as mail-merge letters to suppliers.

4.11 *Extract from Rachel's information for letter-headed paper*

▷ Website

■ Information should concentrate on the number of pages in the site, the details on each page and how they will be linked together. Any **reusable aspects** of a website should also be mentioned.

4.12 Extract from Rachel's information for the website

Information required for my website

My website will contain four pages. The home page will contain the shop's name, logo and a link to each other page.
Each subsequent page will have a consistent layout and style with the shop's name and logo, and be linked back to the home page.
On each of these pages, there will be an image and a list of specific items and prices.My home page will be fixed, as will be the two pages listing details of my usual items for sale (computers and peripherals). The page which will change regularly will be the new stock page.

Coursework Adviser's comments

Good Points
- Rachel has identified the information required.
- Some reusable data has been specified.

Areas for Improvement
- Rachel has only **implied** the links between parts of the solution. She needs to make the links clearer if she is to achieve the highest marks.

▷ Plans

■ Produce at least one diagram. It should be **hand drawn** and **annotated** to explain the layout. It can be used to show the form of the information and how it will be laid out.

■ Plans can also be used to specify further details, such as font size and style, size of the image/logo, format of any text box, colours used or any effects applied.

■ Alternatively, you can use a **series of plans** to convey these details.

4.13 *Extract from Rachel's poster plan*

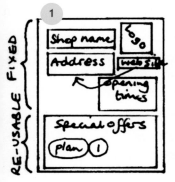
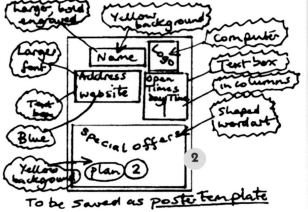

My poster plan
My plan shows how I intend to set out the information. I decided to move the website underneath the address (plan 1). I have added more detail (plan 2) to show how it will be produced. I chose the colours to match my shop and the sizes of fonts to fit the space on the poster.

My website plan

My plan shows how the pages will be hyperlinked together. I have left the 'New Stock' page blank, so it can be reused when new stock arrives. I have added more detail (plan 2) to show how it will be produced. I like the environmental look of the green-grass effect, which conveys a good image. I will copy the shop name, logo and address from the earlier publishing documents. The developed diagram of the home page (plan 2) shows the presentation and the links.

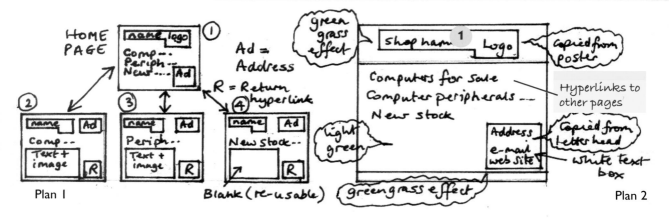

Plan 1   Plan 2

➭ Justification of the chosen software techniques

■ A word-processing package, a desktop publishing package or even a graphics package could be used for a poster. Consider which has the **best features** for your purpose. The **advantages** (and **disadvantages**) could be presented effectively in a table or in words.

Features of a word-processing package that make it suitable to produce my poster

I can type in and save text so I can continue it later. I will need this if I don't finish it in one go. The word processor has a spelling-check feature, which prevents mistakes – however, some of the technical terms I will use in my poster may not be recognised by a spell checker. The word processor has a range of different font names, sizes and styles which I will need to emphasise text. For the opening hours and the address, I will use a larger font size. I intend to use a fancy font style, such as engraved and bold, for the shop name. I can use text boxes to separate sections of my poster – I will use one text box for the special offers and another for the opening hours. This is so that I can move the text boxes around exactly as on my plan. I want my logo to be larger on the poster. I can import and resize it to match the size of the shop name. I will save the basic details on the poster, which remain the same, as a template to reuse again. I need to make sure I don't accidentally overwrite the template.

Disadvantages of a word-processing package

It will do most of what I need, but it doesn't provide an automatic way of moving or resizing some images.

Good Points

- Rachel has justified the features of the chosen software and explained some of them in terms of the needs of the sub-problem.

Areas for Improvement

- She has not identified all the specific features (e.g. image manipulation) which are relevant to the solution.

⇨ Relationships

- Relationships are concerned with **how your sub-problems interrelate**, for example, showing how data used in one solution will be used in other parts by copying and pasting or importing.

- A **logo** may be used on all your publishing documents, and so could provide a simple relationship.

For my poster, the logo will have to be changed to a larger size and it will be at the top right of the poster where it will stand out. I will import and resize it to the same size as the shop name.
I need to make the logo smaller to fit on my letter headed paper, where I am going to place it at the top right of the letter head. I will copy, paste and resize it.

On my website, it will have to be small to fit at the top of each page next to the shop name. I will also use it at the bottom right of the page, with a message next to it to hyperlink back to my home page. I will import and resize it before pasting it onto each web page in turn.

4.16 *Extract from Rachel's relationships*

Good Points

- Rachel has made use of the logo in a limited attempt to link the publishing 'documents' together.
- There is some consistency in styles between the poster, letter-headed paper and website.

Areas for Improvement

- Publishing sub-problems aren't the obvious place to link aspects of a sub-problem together, so Rachel would only obtain a limited mark here.
- Linkage should relate significant parts of data together (e.g. between a database and spreadsheet or using mail merge).

⇨ Test plan

- No specific test plan is needed for publishing. A **test plan** must be produced for design, but may be part of the testing section.

- You may set up a **simple check** if, for example, you have said that your performance criteria for a poster was that four out of five people thought it was attractive, but remember that this is only a **judgement**, not a test.

4.17 *Extract from Rachel's criteria check*

Checking my poster against the criteria I set

<u>What to check:</u> I will check if five people thought my poster was attractive.

<u>How:</u> I will ask five people in my class and record their answers.

	Yes	**No**
Is it colourful?	❏	❏
Is it well laid out?	❏	❏

<u>Expected results:</u> Four out of five people will think my poster is attractive.

<u>Check:</u> Four out of five people from my class answered 'yes' to both questions.

Coursework Adviser's comments

Good Points
- Rachel has attempted to judge how effective her poster was against specific criteria.

Areas for Improvement
- This is not testing as required by the syllabus criteria, so would only receive a low mark, however many times it was repeated.
- Testing should be applied to data where there is an objective result available (e.g. the records shown when a database search is done).

Designing for a database sub-problem

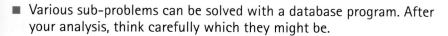

■ Various sub-problems can be solved with a database program. After your analysis, think carefully which they might be.

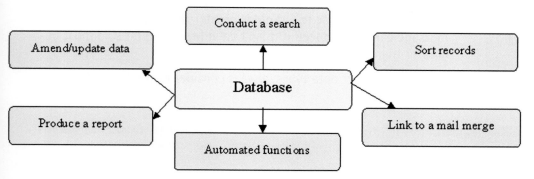

Information required for a database sub-problem

■ For a database, not only do you need to **list the information**, you also have to **consider what will be done with it**. Begin by considering what format the data will take – a key field, text, number, date/time or a memo field, and start to design the structure with field names and types of data.

■ Next think about what will be done to the data:

- Will a data entry screen be needed? Or a data-capture form?

- Will it be sorted? Which field(s)? In what order?

- Will it be searched? Which field(s)? Using what criteria?

- Will a report be needed? Which field(s)? In what sequence?

- Will you need more than one table?

- Will any tables be linked together?

- Will the database link to a mail merge (document or mailing labels)?

Plan of a database

■ Designing a database involves deciding the **form** it will take (the way in which data will need to be displayed). It also involves knowing the underlying structures needed to obtain this. Plan to include a **key field** (which some databases will automatically generate for you).

■ For the solution, consider the **data–entry requirements**.

■ Think about any **sorts** or **searches** that are needed when using it and any reports which will be required.

■ Sometimes your data will need to be **separated** into two or more tables to be manageable.

- Don't forget to consider whether the data will be **linked** together as tables or linked to some other source (i.e. mail merged).

- Begin by designing suitable **field names** – you could abbreviate long names (e.g. 'Price that I will charge' becomes Selling price).

- Think about the types of data – don't forget that you may want it in a specific form (e.g. the specific format for a date could be 'dd/mm/yyyy') or to use a **validation rule**. A validation rule can check that data is within a certain range (e.g. 'Sold is greater than 1'). A validation error message can be produced if it isn't valid (e.g. 'Amount sold must be greater than 1').

- To get the correct data types, always consider **examples of data** you will use.

4.18 *Extract from Rachel's stock information*

Information required for my database

When thinking about my database, I realised that there was too much data for just one table. The data fell into two categories: the stock details and the details about the suppliers. To save duplicating data when I was entering it, I decided that I would enter the **Stock** data and the **Supplier** data separately. This is an important decision, as I will now need to set up two tables.

Information required for my stock

To organise the stock that I need to run 'Bytes for all', I must record these details:

Stock ID (a **key field**), Stock description, Stock type, Date received, Selling price, Cost price, Sold, Re-order level, Amount ordered, Quantity in stock and Supplier ID. Before I think what needs to be done to it, I have shown the data structure shown below:

Field name	Data type	Example
Stock ID	AutoNumber	1
Stock description	Text	P4 1.8Ghz
Stock type	Text	computer
Date received	Date/Time	23/04/2003
Selling price	Currency	£399
Cost price	Currency	£259
Sold	Number	
Re-order level	Number	4
Amount ordered	Number	8
Quantity in stock	Number	12
Supplier ID	Number	2

This will be entered later when I sell items.

- For a reasonable-sized database for your project, you will need several **records**. You can either collect some data to enter (e.g. produce a **data-capture form**) or import data that your teacher may already have. Any data-capture forms used should have the same layout as your database.

Data required to produce the output for the stock table

I have chosen to use a data-entry screen to make sure that data is correctly entered to my stock table. To make it easy, the fields 'Selling price', 'Sold' and 'Quantity in stock' are underneath each other. Here is the screen:

4.19 *Extract from Rachel's data-entry screen*

Stock ID		1	Stock description		P4 1.8Ghz

Stock type	computer	Date received	23/04/2003
Selling price	£399.00	Cost price	£259.00
Sold			
Quantity in stock	12	Re-order level	4
Amount ordered	8	Supplier ID	2

■ Plan some **searches** and say why you are searching for these records (e.g. 'I need to find all the printers that are in stock'). Think of a name for the search (e.g. 'Stock type').

Information to output as a search

I want to check the stock that 'Bytes for all' has in. I will need to select certain types of stock. I have shown the search conditions here to find all the printers. There may be a better way to use the search so that I can find any item by its type. If there were a simpler way to do this, I would use it.

4.20 *Extract from Rachel's search for printers*

Field	**Stock type**
Table	**Stock**
Show	✔
Sort	
Criteria	**'printer'**

■ Plan some **sorts** – explain why you are sorting the records (e.g. 'display all stock in the order received, to see which stock was received first). Think of a name for the sort (e.g. 'Oldest stock').

Information to output as a sort

I want a list sorted in date order (when the stock was received) so I can see which is the oldest stock. I have shown the sort conditions to find the stock in date order.

4.21 *Extract from Rachel's sort into date order*

Field	**Date received**
Table	**Stock**
Show	✔
Sort	**Ascending**
Criteria	

⇨ Form of the output

■ Plan a **report** – say why you are going to use the report and what form it will take. Reports can be in columns or tables. They improve the presentation of your printout. You could plan a report to show some of the stock details and call it 'Stock types'.

4.22 *Extract from Rachel's stock report*

Information to output as a report

I want to display for the bank manager all the stock that 'Bytes for all' has. He only needs to see certain fields. The list needs to contain: Stock description, Stock type, Date received, Selling price and Quantity in stock. I have shown the plan of the report below:

Stock description	Stock type	Date received	Selling price	Quantity in stock
–	–	–	–	–

4.23 *Extract from Rachel's Suppliers table*

Information required for my Suppliers table

Having decided to separate the stock details from the suppliers, I need to record their details, which are: Supplier ID, Company name, Address1, Address2 and Postcode. I will choose to import the data from a previous AQA task. This will make the data entry quicker and simpler. I have shown the data structure below:

Field name	Data type	Example
Supplier ID	AutoNumber	2
Company name	Text	*Fresniere Computers Ltd*
Address1	Text	*22 Cromwell Road*
Address2	Date/Time	*Bramley*
Post Code	Number	*BR7 6TL*

Coursework Adviser's comments

Good Points

- Rachel has identified the **main forms** and **underlying structures** of the database design.

Areas for Improvement

- She has not identified any of the activities required of the supplier database.
- There has been little consideration of the user's needs.

⇨ Relationships

■ **Linking** together two (or more) tables is particularly useful to avoid having to enter data more than once (called **data duplication**). Linked tables must have the **same field name** in each table; for example, the stock table shown earlier has a field name called Supplier ID. As long as there is a field name also called Supplier ID in the Suppliers table, the two tables can be linked together. You could also link the database to mail-merge letters.

Linking my tables together

I will have two tables to prevent my data having to be entered more than once. It will reduce the chance of making mistakes. One table is for my stock and the other for the supplier's details. I can link the tables together to enable me to print details from both tables. To link them, the tables must have one common field (I will call it Supplier ID). I have shown the plan of the links here:

4.24 *Extract from Rachel's linked tables*

Stock
Field name
Stock ID
Stock description
Stock type
Date received
Selling price
Cost price
Sold
Re-order level
Amount ordered
Quantity in stock
Supplier ID

Suppliers
Field name
Supplier ID
Company name
Address1
Address2
Postcode

Coursework Adviser's comments

Good Points
- Rachel has identified a significant link between aspects of the sub-problem.

Areas for Improvement
- As the design has developed, she hasn't thought about **more complex searches or sorts**. This is one aspect of database use which allows more confident candidates to demonstrate their knowledge.

4.25 *Extract from Rachel's mail-merge letters*

I will write letters to my suppliers ordering items of stock which I am short of. I will set up a search of the database which links all the items which are understocked to the suppliers' table. The letter will use my letter head which I designed previously. It will include linked fields from each database table to re-order stock items below the re-order level.

My letterhead

<Company name>
<Address1>
<Address2>
<Post Code>

These are the field names in **black** which I plan to merge with the database.

Dear Stock Manager of <Company name>

Please supply

Stock description	*Stock type*	*Cost price*	*Amount*
<Stock description>	<Stock type>	<Cost price>	<Amount ordered>

Yours …

⇨ Justification of using the database

- Consider which features of the database software you will use and **explain** them in terms of the sub-problem to be solved.

4.26 *Extract from Rachel's justification of the software*

Justifying the database software

The database allows me to use and change field names (which are up to 15 characters long). It offers a range of data types, such as **text** (for most fields), **memo** (for longer data), **number** (whole numbers, decimal numbers, currency, etc.) or **dates** (e.g. 01/01/01, 01 Jan 2001, etc.). The field length can be changed. It is easy to change data in a field, which I will need when I reuse the data. I can set it to a default value for every field. I can customise the field layout. I can set up a **validation rule** to make sure data is entered as I want.

I can carry out simple searches (e.g. **Stock type** is equal to **printer**) or more complex ones (e.g. Quantity is less than 3 AND Stock type is equal to printer).

Sorts are easy to do in the database (e.g. sort every record by the **Date received** in ascending order).

I can create a report which chooses only certain fields, presented in a different order to the original set-up. Another feature of the database that I will need is to mail-merge with a standard letter. This is so I can send individual letters to any supplier of my shop.

Coursework Adviser's comments

Good Points
- Rachel has identified software features which are relevant to the solution.

Areas for Improvement
- She hasn't explained what the features will be used to do.

⇨ Test plan

- Designing a **test plan** for your database is essential. In Rachel's case, she has done the design, but chosen to include it in the Testing section (see page 168). Remember that a design is not complete without a test plan.

Designing for a spreadsheet sub-problem

⇨ Information required for a spreadsheet sub-problem

- List the **information** needed for the spreadsheet and consider what will be done to it. Begin by considering what **format** the data will take – headings or text, numbers of various types (integers, numbers to a certain number of decimal places or currency) and dates.

- Design the **spreadsheet structure** with column and row headings and consider any **calculations** which are needed. Think about the maths you will use.

- Think about what will be done to the data:

  - Will calculations be done to it?

  - What formula(e) may be needed?

  - Will it be sorted? If so, on which column(s) and using what criteria?

  - Will any graphs be needed? For which column(s)? What type of chart?

  - Will data entry need to be validated?

  - Will the results from any calculation be used in future spreadsheets?

  - Will the data be imported from any other source?

4.27 *Extract from Rachel's section on information required*

Information required for my spreadsheet
I will have separate parts of my spreadsheet for the sales and the payments. For the sales part, I will copy the details of stock sold from the database. I will add formulae to calculate the total value for each item. For the payments part, I will enter the amounts for electricity, rent and rates per week. I will input the wages that I will have to pay. I will include a formula to work out the total sales, total payments and profit/loss each week.

Reusing the spreadsheet
When I have set up and tested the first spreadsheet, I will copy and paste the necessary parts of it into worksheets for the next few weeks. I will use a formula to make sure that the end of week profit/loss is transferred as the start balance for the next week.

⇨ Plan of a spreadsheet

- Designing a spreadsheet involves planning the **form** it will take (the way in which data will need to be displayed) and also knowing the **underlying structures** needed to obtain this.

- Plan to include an **initial outline** with the headings and any fixed data shown.

- At the next stage of planning, include the **formulae** you need – always save time and effort by recognising when a formula can be **replicated** (copied) down a column or across a row.

- Show the type of data needed (especially numeric).

- A further stage could be to indicate when columns or rows might need the width or height changing. Think about **'special' values** which will benefit from being emphasised in some way (with borders and shading).

4.28 *Extract from Rachel's spreadsheet plans*

Plan 1, showing the form of the output.

The data to be copied from the Stock table, showing items sold

	A	B	C	D	E		H
1	Bytes for all: sales and Payments spreadsheet						
2	Sales this week		09/05/03				
3	Stock ID	Stock description	Stock type	Date received	Selling price	Cost price	Sold	Total
4	1	P4 1.8GHz	computer	23/04/2003	£399.00	£ 259.00	4	
5	2	P4 2.0GHz	computer	02/05/2003	£459.00	£ 359.00	3	
6	3	P4 2.3GHz	computer	10/03/2003	£579.00	£ 459.00	3	
7						TOTAL		
8	Payments						
9							per week
10	Electricity						£ 58.50
11	Rent						£ 250.00
12	Rates						£ 135.00
13	Wages	First name	Last name	hours	per hour	Gross pay	
14		Jane	Byte	35	£ 12.00	£ 420.00	
15		Dave	Ramm	35	£ 9.50	£ 332.50	
16		Alan	Memory	8	£ 3.50	£ 28.00	
17		Sue	Simms	20	£ 7.50	£ 150.00	
18							
19						TOTAL	
20						PROFIT	

I have set the date to be the same format as in the Stock table.

Plan 2, showing the data transferred and the formulae needed.

		D	E	F	G	H
3	Stock description	Stock type	Date received	Selling price	Cost price	Sold	Total
4	4	P4 1.8GHz	computer	37734	399	259	4	=(E4-F4)*G4
5	5	P4 2.0GHz	computer	37743	459	359	3	=(E5-F5)*G5
6	6	P4 2.3GHz	computer	37690	579	459	4	=(E6-F6)*G6
7						TOTAL	=SUM(H4:H6)
8	Payments						

Plan 3, showing the formulae for the wages and changes in column widths.

	B	C	D	E	F
13	First name	Last name	hours	per hour	amount
14	Jane	Byte	35	12	=D14*E14
15	Dave	Ramm	35	9.5	=D15*E15

⇨ Justify using the spreadsheet

■ Consider which **features** of the spreadsheet you will use after checking your plan. Explain them in terms of the sub-problem to be solved.

4.29 Extract from Rachel's reasons for choosing the spreadsheet

Reasons for choosing the spreadsheet

It lets me organise data into rows and columns, which I need for the sales and payments. It lets me change the height of the rows and width of the columns. I need the row for the spreadsheet title to be larger and the column widths for the names must be wider to fit them in. I can add extra rows or columns if I need to extend the spreadsheet. I don't know that I will need this, but my plan may not have considered everything.

I can change the type of data for numbers – into integers, to a number of decimal places or use currency when I need to. The spreadsheet even has an automatic button to change numbers into currency. I will certainly need to use this for the money.

I can align words for headings and text at the left, right or centre of a cell. I plan to centre the headings so they look correct compared with the numbers.

I can adjust the size of the font to fit in a cell. I can highlight it and change the style to bold, underlined or italic. Main headings (e.g. **Sales**) will be in bold. I can fill cells in colour and include borders. The profit/loss and the totals will be filled in yellow to match the colour scheme used on my poster.

I can print a page in portrait or landscape, and I can adjust the margins to fit on a page. I want the page to be able to fit in portrait as it gives me more space to fit extra sales and payments.

I can copy data and past it in from a database – this is to make sure it is accurate and save retyping. I plan to run a search which identifies stock sold, then copy and paste it each week.

I can easily use a simple formula – by pressing the = sign and typing in the formula (e.g. = B14 * C14). This is needed for all the totals and amounts. There are some formulae which can be used by pressing a button (e.g. **= SUM(E3:E9)**). I will need the SUM formula to find the total of the sales and payments. To make things easy to enter and make sure I reduce the chance of a mistake, I can replicate formulae down a column. I will use this for the sales.

I can use an absolute formula (i.e. $A$4) to fix a cell, if the same cell has to be used for every formula. I can print formulae out to check that I have used the correct one.

▷ Relationships

- Explain how the data used in the database is transferred to the spreadsheet, or between spreadsheets.

4.30 *Extract from Rachel's relationships*

Relationships

My spreadsheet will **accept data** already typed in to the stock database and checked there. I will find all new sales and copy them. Within my spreadsheet, I will use separate worksheets for each week's finances. I will set up a **template** for the week's finances, with headings and formulae, and **copy it** for subsequent weeks. The end-of-week **balance** will automatically **be copied forward** to start the next week using a formula.

▷ Test plan

- Designing a **test plan** for your spreadsheet is essential. In Rachel's case, she has done the design, but chosen to include it in the testing section. Remember that a design is not complete without a test plan.

UNIT 3: IMPLEMENTATION

SESSION 1

Implementing publishing sub-problems

■ Capture **screen shots** of your work at all the key stages. It will make it easier to explain what you did and how you did it.

4.31 Extract from Rachel's publishing implementation – poster

Implementing my poster (1)
I have shown three stages (1, 2 and 3) in the production of my poster and explained how I produced it.

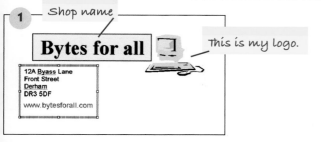

Annotation of my work

First, I put in the shop name at the top of the poster. Then I copied and pasted the logo to the right of the shop name, before resizing it. I decided to group together the name and logo so that I could move and resize them more easily until I had got them into the best position. I have shown how I included a text box for the address underneath the shop's name. I left out the phone number, as I wanted people to visit the shop. I removed the border around the text box. The font size was increased to 16 points, as shown in my plan, so it would stand out and be readable from a distance.

I have added another text box showing the opening times. I left a border around it, so it is a separate part of the poster and not linked to the shop name and logo. I have shown how I have moved the word art for special offers into place. The fixed data is only taking up about half the space on the poster.

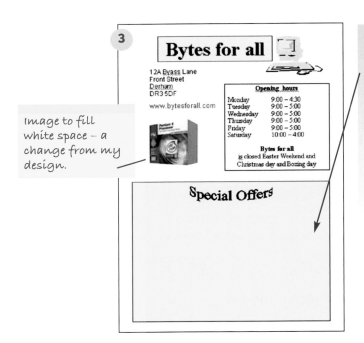

3

In this version, I have added a blank frame for the special offers. The frame has been coloured in yellow similar to the background for the shop's name. The poster has been saved as 'poster template'.

Image to fill white space – a change from my design.

Implementing my poster (2)

I opened my poster template, which I had saved in 'Read only' form so I couldn't accidentally save over it. I have completed it for the first time and shown the special offers. I typed the new details into the blank text box and imported the clip art picture of a printer. The price of computers was emphasised in a separate text box with a white background. The finished poster is exactly as I expected it to be. Originally I had thought that one third of the A4 sheet would be enough for the special offers. The amount of space for the special offers as been increased to closer to half rather than one-third, as it fits the space better. This is because the balance between the reusable and fixed data looks better this way, and I anticipate that I will always need the extra space for new stock.

4.31 *continued*

Implementing my letter head

I have shown three stages in the production of my letter head and explained how I produced it.

1

4.32 *Extract from Rachel's publishing implementation – letter-headed paper*

As in my plan, I have started by copying the shop name and logo from the poster. I have resized it and made it smaller to fit across the top of the page.

To the left of the name and logo, I have added a text box, so I can enter the address of shop. Underneath I have included the e-mail address and, below that, the website. The e-mail address is in blue and underlined as the plan shows.

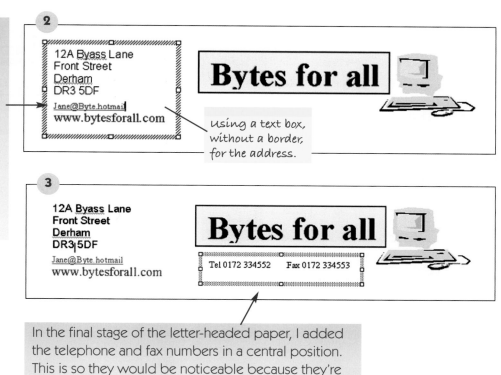

Using a text box, without a border, for the address.

In the final stage of the letter-headed paper, I added the telephone and fax numbers in a central position. This is so they would be noticeable because they're immediately underneath the shop name.

Implementing my website

I have shown five stages in the production of my website and explained how I produced it.

4.33 *Extract from Rachel's publishing implementation – website*

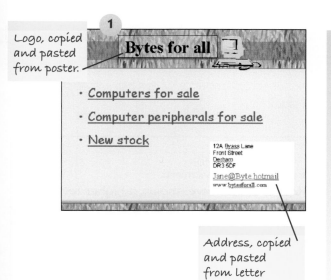

Logo, copied and pasted from poster.

Address, copied and pasted from letter head.

Here, I have shown my website's home page. I chose the design template to fit with my design. It looked relaxing and would encourage people to shop at **Bytes for all**. The shop name and logo is on the title bar, copied and pasted from the poster and resized to fit. The address details are in a text box at the bottom right-hand side – copied and pasted from the letter-head paper so I made no mistakes. There are three other pages which I have also created. The home page shows the hyperlinks to them. I highlighted the web page name (e.g. Computers for sale) and made sure it was hyperlinked to that web page. I repeated this for each web page.

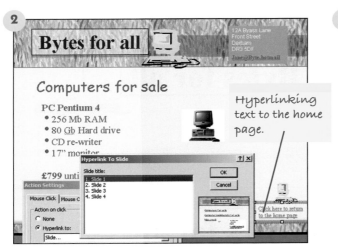

2

This shows the hyperlink back to my home page from the text message. I copied this message to each page to make it more efficient.

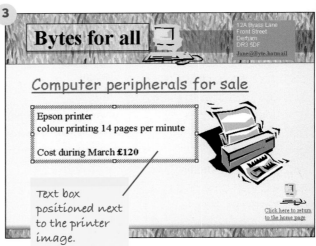

3

I have added a text box to allow me to put the text next to the picture of the printer.

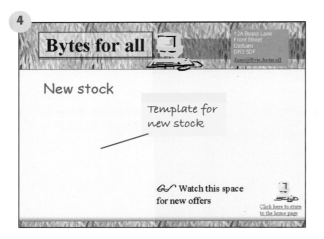

4

This is the page which I saved as a template for the new stock. Part of the page is reusable, as it changes regularly.

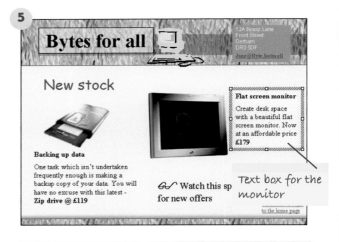

5

I have shown the addition of a text box about the flat-screen monitor which has just arrived in stock.

Coursework Adviser's comments

Good Points

- Although the implementation has to be judged overall, for this section Rachel has shown a good level of skill and understanding. She achieved this by explaining how they were implemented.
- Copying and resizing the shop name and logo on the letter head and website demonstrates efficiency, as does copying the return hyperlink to other pages.

Areas for Improvement

- Rachel could have shown a higher level of skill and understanding by explaining the stages to produce the final outcome in more detail. For example, there is no reference to importing the hyperlink (computer) clip art, nor how the spectacles were included in the 'Watch this space ...' text in Stage 4 above.

Implementing database sub-problems

⇨ **Implement the database structure**

- Set up the **field names** and **data types** identified in the design plan.

- You may need to follow some or all of these stages:
  - Add the data to be used – import it or type it in.
  - Create a data-capture form.
  - Print out the complete database.
  - Set up any sorts, searches or reports to be done and print them.
  - Make changes to the data (**reuse** the database).
  - Print out the database again.
  - Rerun the sorts, searches and reports and print them out.

4.34 *Extract from Rachel's database set up*

The fields for my stock table

In the database, I will set up a new stock table with these fields: Stock ID (a **key field** using AutoNumber), Stock description (text), Stock type (drop-down menu), Date received (date field), Selling price, Cost price (both currency), Sold, Re-order level, Amount ordered, Quantity in stock and Supplier ID (all numbers). The Stock type is a change from my design. I have shown the field details here.

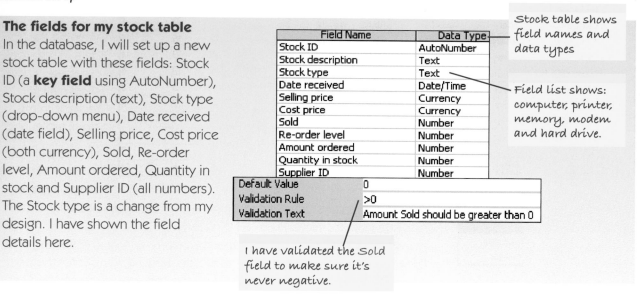

Stock table shows field names and data types

Field list shows: computer, printer, memory, modem and hard drive.

I have validated the Sold field to make sure it's never negative.

4.35 *Extract from Rachel's data-capture form set-up*

A data-capture form

I decided the logical order for the fields. I ensured the Stock type was a drop-down field to make data entry even quicker. Below, I have shown the data-capture form being used to enter a record. I will print out a blank form to use for paper-based data collection. I placed **Selling price**, **Sold** and **Quantity in stock** underneath each other, as they would change most often.

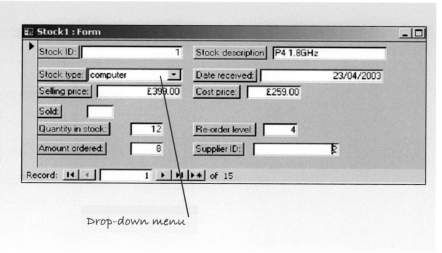

Drop-down menu

Using a data-entry form

The Stock ID is a key field, automatically generated. The **Stock type** is a choice from a **drop-down** menu. This was a change from my design, but it was more efficient to use. The Stock description takes longest to type in, as it's all text.

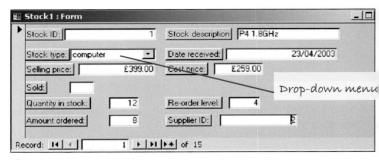

4.36 *Extract from Rachel's data-capture form use*

Stock ID	Stock description	Stock type	Date received	Selling price	Cost price	Sold	Re-order	Amount	Quantity	Supplier ID
1	P4 1.8GHz	computer	23/04/2003	£399.00	£259.00		4	8	12	2
2	P4 2.0GHz	computer	02/05/2003	£469.00	£359.00		3	8	1	2
3	P4 2.3GHz	computer	10/03/2003	£579.00	£459.00		3	6	8	7
4	Epson 62B	printer	23/03/2003	£69.99	£49.99		2	12	12	4
5	HP Deskjet 90	printer	02/05/2003	£125.00	£79.00		7	6	12	3
6	Canon 340C	printer	10/03/2003	£109.99	£69.99		5	8	20	5
7	128Kb RAM	memory	12/03/2003	£25.00	£10.00		6	10	15	14
8	256Kb RAM	memory	12/03/2003	£45.00	£18.00		6	12	20	14
9	Maxtor 80Gb HD	hard drive	15/03/2003	£95.00	£45.00		5	15	10	8
10	19" Monitor liama	monitor	20/03/2003	£225.00	£125.00		2	5	8	9
11	15" TFT Mitsubisi	monitor	21/03/2003	£259.00	£129.00		3	5	2	8
12	Maxtor 120Gb HD	hard drive	22/03/2003	£119.00	£58.00		5	12	4	8
13	17" TFT Mitsubisi	monitor	23/03/2003	£299.00	£149.00		2	5	7	8
14	P4 2.5GHz	computer	30/03/2003	£999.00	£599.00		3	8	5	7
15	L&G 56k	modem	01/04/2003	£59.00	£29.00		5	5	6	11

4.37 *Extract from Rachel's stock table*

Viewing the data in my stock database: I have shown all 15 records in my stock table.

I made it simple to enter the **stock type** by choosing from a list. This is more efficient for the user. I had all the main stock items in the list.

The **Date received** field was in the form dd/mm/yyyy. The **Selling** and **Cost** prices were quick to enter, as I just entered a number for the price – the £ sign and pence were added by the software because I had set the data type to currency. I have yet to enter any sales in the **Sold** field.

4.38 *Extract from Rachel's search for printers*

Implementing a search for stock

I need to find all the printers. In my plan, I was going to type the stock name into a design each time. This would be confusing for a user. I set up a parameter search, which allows a user to choose the stock when the search is run (1).

This is what happens as I run it (2).

This is the result of my search for printers shown here (3).

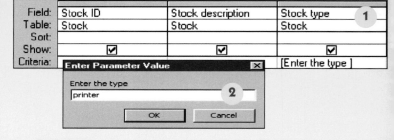

	Stock ID	Stock description	Stock type	Date received	Selling price	Quantity
▶	4	Epson 62B	printer	23/03/2003	£89.99	12
3	5	HP Deskjet 90	printer	02/05/2003	£125.00	12
	6	Canon 340C	printer	10/03/2003	£109.99	20

Stock type	Date received
Stock	Stock
	Ascending
☑	☑

I have set the sort to Ascending.

This is part of the sorted printout.

Stock ID	Stock description	Stock type	Date received	Supplier ID
6	Canon 340C	printer	10/03/2003	5
3	P4 2.3GHz	computer	10/03/2003	7
8	256Kb RAM	memory	12/03/2003	14
7	128Kb RAM	memory	12/03/2003	14
9	Maxtor 80Gb HD	hard drive	15/03/2003	8
10	19" Monitor liama	monitor	20/03/2003	9

4.39 *Extract from Rachel's setting up of a sort*

Setting up a sort of old stock

I only need to show certain fields when I sort the stock into the date received. I want to display records in ascending order, so the oldest stock is at the top of the list.

4.40 *Extract from Rachel's new table*

Suppliers : Table	
Field Name	**Data Type**
Supplier ID	AutoNumber
Company name	Text
Address1	Text
Address3	Text
Post Code	Text

Setting up a table of suppliers

I have entered the field names and data types. Next, I have added the data. So I didn't spend a long time typing it in, I have imported data from a previous AQA assignment. My teacher made this available for me to save time checking that the data was correct.

4.41 *Extract from Rachel's links between tables*

Here are my two tables with the fields, Supplier ID, linked together.

Setting up a relationship between the suppliers and stock databases

I need to link the tables together to be able to produce mail-merge letters to suppliers. The link will associate every supplier code in the stock table to the correct supplier name and address in the Supplier table. I just displayed the two tables and dragged the field (Supplier ID) from the Stock table to the Suppliers table. The line shows the link between the two tables.

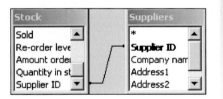

Each table is selected along this row.

Stock description	Stock type	Selling price	Date received	Quantity in stock	Company name	Address1
Stock	Stock	Stock	Stock	Stock	Suppliers	Suppliers
☑	☑	☑	☑	☑	☑	☑
	[Type]					

4.42 *Extract from Rachel's search for stock of a certain type*

Oldest stock
Re-orders
Stock type
Supplier order

Enter Parameter Value ☒ 1

Type of stock

printer

OK   Cancel

Getting a printout of the same types of stock to check the supplier

I have shown the search (1) to find all the printers in stock.

I have included the results of the search (2), linking data from both the Stock and Suppliers tables.

Stock description	Stock type	Selling price	Date received	Quantity in stock	Company name	Address1	Address2	Post Code
Epson 626	printer	£89.99	23/03/2003	12	Bennett plc	4 School Terrace	Leeds	LA7 2VW
HP Deskjet 90	printer	£125.00	02/05/2003	20	Artez Co	51 Camam Court	Sheffield	S13 7DI
Canon 340C	printer	£109.99	10/03/2003	20	Berglund Bros	6 Castle Road	Bramley	BR7 4TB

4.43 *Extract from Rachel's mail merge for out-of-stock items*

Re-ordering under-stocked items

To find out-of-stock items, I made a search for items where the **Re-order level** was greater than the **Quantity in stock.** I made sure I re-ordered it from the correct supplier by linking my two tables (**Stock** and **Suppliers**) together.

I have shown my search (1) for items where the **Re-order level** was greater than the **Quantity in stock.** I have printed out the under-stocked items (2) linked to the supplier.

1

Stock description	Stock type	Cost price	Quantity in stock	Re-order level	Amount ordered	Company name	Address1
Stock	Stock	Stock	Stock	Stock	Stock	Suppliers	Suppliers
☑	☑	☑	☑	☑	☑	☑	☑
				>[Quantity in stock]			

2

Re-orders : Select Query

Stock ID	Stock description	Stock type	Cost price	Quantity	Re-order	Amount	Company name	Address1	Address2	Post Code
	P4 2.0GHz	computer	£359.00	2	3	8	Fresniere Computers	22 Cromwell Road	Bramley	BR7 6TL
11	15" TFT Mitsubisi	monitor	£129.00	2	3	5	Wong Supplies	43 Sandwich Road	Sheffield	S13 1EE
*	)Number)									

The red underline shows the word processor doesn't recognise proper nouns in the address.

3

12A Byass Lane
Front Street
Derham
DR3 5DF
Jane@Byte.hotmail
www.bytesforall.com

Bytes for all

Tel 0172 334552   Fax 0172 334553

Fields from my database used in the mail merge.

«Company_name»
«Address1»
«Address2»
«Post_Code»

Dear Stock Manager of «Company_name»

Please supply:

Stock description   Stock type   Cost price   Amount ordered
«Stock_description» «Stock_type» «Cost_price»   «Amount_ordered»

Yours sincerely

Ms Byte
Bytes for all

To make easy to remember, I called my search for any under-stocked items **Re-orders**. Next, I linked my database fields with the letter-head paper which I produced to advertise the shop. I set up a template (3) and linked it to the search called **Re-orders**.

This shows the fields I have linked from the two tables. I have used my letter head which I produced in the publishing section of my project.

4

12A Byass Lane
Front Street
Derham
DR3 5DF

Jane@Byte.hotmail
www.bytesforall.com

Bytes for all

Tel 0172 334552   Fax 0172 334553

I have shown two of the results (4 and 5) after running my mail merge.

Fresniere Computers Ltd
22 Cromwell Road
Bromley
BR7 6TL

Dear Stock Manager of Fresniere Computers Ltd

Please supply:

Stock description	Stock type	Cost price	Amount ordered
P4 2.0 GHz	computer	£359.00	8

Yours sincerely

Ms Byte
Bytes for all

5

12A Byass Lane
Front Street
Derham
DR3 5DF

Jane@Byte.hotmail
www.bytesforall.com

Bytes for all

Tel 0172 334552   Fax 0172 334553

Wong Supplies
43 Sandwich Road
Sheffield
S13 1EE

Dear Stock Manager of Wong Supplies

Please supply:

Stock description	Stock type	Cost price	Amount ordered
15" TFT Mitsubisi	monitor	£129.00	6

Yours sincerely

Ms Byte
Bytes for all

Coursework Adviser's comments
Good Points
- Rachel has shown a good level of skill and understanding by annotating the search, linkage of tables and mail-merge fields.

Areas for Improvement
- If the table had been updated to show the reusability of the database and the mail-merge re-run, Rachel would have a strong case for being awarded very high marks.

Implementing spreadsheet sub-problems

⇨ **Set up the spreadsheet template and formulae**

- The following steps are useful when setting up a **template**:
  - Add the data to be used initially.
  - Print out the complete spreadsheet.
  - Add and print out all the formulae.
  - Make changes to the data (reuse the spreadsheet).
  - Print out the spreadsheet again.
  - Develop a version for the next period of time.

- Check your **performance criteria** and ensure the **form of the output** is correct – choose portrait or landscape, with or without gridlines. You may choose to print only certain columns.

- Displaying all the **formulae** you have used in the design is essential if you are to obtain marks for efficiency and understanding. Explain how you **entered** or **replicated** the formula.

- **Copying and pasting** the model for future time periods is a way of bringing in **reusability** and showing **efficiency**.

- Make several changes to the data and reprint the spreadsheet each time – show it over a period of time. Always **annotate** the changes you make. Use **screen shots** to help show your development.

4.44 *Extract from Rachel's spreadsheet model of profit/loss*

I followed my plan and copied the data from my database into the spreadsheet in the sales section. Next, I typed in a formula (=(E4–F4)*G4) to work out the total value of each sale. I replicated it down the rest of the sales. I typed in a formula (=D14*E14) for the Gross pay and also replicated that down the rest of the employees.

	A	B	C	D	E	F	G	H
1	Bytes for all: sales and Payments spreadsheet							
2	Sales this week		09/05/03					
3	Stock ID	Stock description	Stock type	Date received	Selling price	Cost price	Sold	Total
4	1	P4 1.8GHz	computer	23/04/2003	£399.00	£ 259.00	4	£ 560.00
5	2	P4 2.0GHz	computer	02/05/2003	£459.00	£ 359.00	3	£ 300.00
6	3	P4 2.3GHz	computer	10/03/2003	£579.00	£ 459.00	3	£ 360.00
7						TOTAL		£ 1,220.00
8	Payments							
9								per week
10	Electricity							£ 58.50
11	Rent							£ 250.00
12	Rates							£ 135.00
13	Wages	First name	Last name	hours	per hour	Gross pay		
14		Jane	Byte	35	£ 12.00	£ 420.00		
15		Dave	Ramm	35	£ 9.50	£ 332.50		
16		Alan	Memory	8	£ 3.50	£ 28.00		
17		Sue	Simms	20	£ 7.50	£ 150.00		
18								£ 930.50
19						TOTAL		£ 1,374.00
20							PROFIT	£ 154.00

This is the query to show stock sold. I copied the data and pasted it into the empty cells (in A4) in my spreadsheet.

Transfer to S/S: Select Query

	Stock ID	Stock description	Stock type	Date received	Selling price	Cost price	Sold
▶	1	P4 1.8GHz	computer	23/04/2003	£399.00	£259.00	4
	2	P4 2.0GHz	computer	02/05/2003	£459.00	£359.00	3
	3	P4 2.3GHz	computer	10/03/2003	£579.00	£459.00	3

4.45 *Extract from Rachel's spreadsheet formulae*

	A	B	C	D	E	F	G	H
1	Bytes fo							
2	Sales this		37869					
3		Stock description	Stock type	Date received	Selling price	Cost price	Sold	Total
4	4	P4 1.8GHz	computer	37734	399	259	4	=(E4-F4)*G4
5	5	P4 2.0GHz	computer	37743	459	359	3	=(E5-F5)*G5
6	6	P4 2.3GHz	computer	37690	579	459	4	=(E6-F6)*G6
7						TOTAL		=SUM(H4:H6)
8	Payments							
9								per week
10	Electricity							58.5
11	Rent							250
12	Rates							135
13	Wages	First name	Last name	hours	per hour	amount		
14		Jane	Byte	35	12	=D14*E14		
15		Dave	Ramm	35	9.5	=D15*E15		
16		Alan	Memory	8	3.5	=D16*E16		
17		Sue	Simms	20	7.5	=D17*E17		
18						=SUM(F14:F17)		
19								=SUM(H10:H18)
20								=H7-H19

I replicated this formula from H4 to H6.

I used the SUM formula to add up H4, H5 and H6.

I replicated this formula from F14 to F17.

I used the SUM formula for these amounts.

I subtracted the payments from the sales.

4.46 *Extract from Rachel's spreadsheet for next week*

I added a formula to copy the profit/loss from the previous week by pressing = and clicking on last week's profit/loss.

	A	B	C	D	E	F	G	H
1	Bytes for							
2	Sales this w							
3							start balance -£	154.00
4	Stock ID	Stock description	Stock type	Date received	Selling price	Cost price	Sold	Total
5	4	Epson 62B	printer	23/04/2003	£ 89.99	£45.99	2	£ 88.00
6	5	HP Deskjet	printer	02/05/2003	£ 125.00	£79.00	7	£ 322.00
7	6	Canon 340C	printer	10/03/2003	£ 109.99	£65.99	5	£ 220.00
8	3	P4 2.3GHz	computer	10/03/2003	£ 579.00	£ 459.00	5	£ 600.00
9								
10								£ 1,076.00
11	Payments							
12								per week
13	Electricity							£ 52.00
14	Rent							£ 250.00
15	Rates							£ 135.00
16	Wages	First name	Last name	hours	per hour	Gross pay		
17		Jane	Byte	35	£ 12.00	£ 420.00		
18		Dave	Ramm	30	£ 9.50	£ 285.00		
19		Alan	Memory	8	£ 3.50	£ 28.00		
20		Sue	Simms	12	£ 7.50	£ 90.00		
21								£ 823.00
							TOTAL	£ 1,260.00
							PROFIT	-£ 184.00

I had to change my formula to include the start balance. I also inserted some extra rows, as I realised that I hadn't left enough space for several items sold.

I changed the number of hours worked by Dave and Sue. The formula correctly changed their Gross pay.

Coursework Adviser's comments

Good Points

- For this stage, Rachel has shown a good level of skill and understanding by annotating the formulae used.
- Rachel shows the linkage between the database and spreadsheet, and recognises a design fault in the number of rows left blank.

Areas for Improvement

- Although there has been some updating of the data to show the reusability of the spreadsheet, Rachel hasn't shown the start balance formula and considered that it is actually a loss, not a profit.

UNIT 4: TESTING

SESSION 1 — Testing database sub-problems

▷ The testing plan

- There are several aspects of a database which should be tested. You will need to check that:
  - The **data entry** stage works
  - The **processes** done to the database work

- Begin with a **test plan**. Make a list of everything you need to test. For each test, think about:
  - what is being tested?
  - what test data you will use?
  - how you will do it?
  - what are the expected results?

4.47 *Extract from Rachel's testing plan*

My test plan for the stock table

I decided that simplest way to show my test plan was to use a table. This would mean that I didn't have to type out lots of words for each test and I wouldn't forget any important parts of the test. When I had designed my test plan, I would carry out the tests and compare the results with what I expected them to be. If any were different, I would check which was correct and sort it out. Although I know that my test plan is part of my design, I have decided to keep it together with my test printouts to make it clearer to show that my tests work.

Test	What I am testing	How I will do it	Test data	Expected results
1	Data entry test. Does it accept an extreme date?	Type a new item of stock with that date	31/12/2003	It should be accepted
2	Data entry test. Does it accept a type of stock that I don't keep?	Add a new item of stock from the drop-down menu	A speaker	It should be rejected
3	Data entry test. Does it accept invalid data?	Enter a negative number in Sold field	-1	It should be rejected with a suitable message

4	Process test Can my sort show the most recent stock at the top of the list	Choose the field date received and sort in descending order	All the data in my stock table	From the top: HP Deskjet 02/05/2003 P4 2.0GHz 02/05/2003 .... P4 2.3GHz 10/03/2003
5	Process test Does it find all the memory?	Run my search called Stock type	Memory	It should show ID Stock type 7 128k memory 8 256k memory
6	Process test Does it find all the stock items which need re-ordering?	Run my search called Re-orders	Is Re-order level greater than Quantity in stock	It should show Desc. Re-ord Quant P4 2.0GHz 1 3 15" TFT Mitsubisi 2 3 Maxtor 120Gb HD 4 5

Coursework Adviser's comments

Good Points
- Rachel's test plan is in a form which makes it easy to include all the required aspects.

Areas for Improvement
- The plan is limited to setting up a test for only a few parts of the solution. A comprehensive test plan should refer to all data-entry stages which can be tested and all essential processes which have to take place.

▷ The testing stage

■ It is good practice to print out **several versions** of the complete database. When you need to show the expected results for a sort, just **number** them on the printout and **label** it. If you need to show the results of a search, just **highlight** them on the printout and label it.

Testing my plan works
To make it easier to show expected results, I have printed out my table after making changes. I could just highlight the expected results to save time in typing them out. I have checked each test and compared it with the expected results.

4.48 *Extract from Rachel's Database testing stage*

Stock ID	Stock description	Stock type	Date received	Selling price	Cost price	Re-order level	Amount ordered	Quantity in stock	Supplier ID
1	P4 1.8GHz	computer	23/04/2003	£399.00	£259.00	4	8	12	2
2	P4 2.0GHz	computer	02/05/2003	£459.00	£359.00	3	8	1	2
3	P4 2.3GHz	computer	10/03/2003	£579.00	£459.00	3	6	8	7
4	Epson 62B	printer	23/03/2003	£89.99	£49.99	2	12		4
5	HP Deskjet 90	printer	02/05/2003	£125.00	£79.00	7	6		3
6	Canon 340C	printer	10/03/2003	£109.99	£69.99	5	8		5
7	128Kb RAM	memory	12/03/2003	£25.00	£10.00	6	10		14
8	256Kb RAM	memory	12/03/2003	£45.00	£18.00	6	12	20	14
9	Maxtor 80Gb HD	hard drive	15/03/2003	£95.00	£45.00	5	15	10	8
10	19" Monitor liama	monitor	20/03/2003	£225.00	£125.00	2	5	8	9
11	15" TFT Mitsubisi	monitor	21/03/2003	£259.00	£129.00	3	5	2	8
12	Maxtor 120Gb HD	hard drive	22/03/2003	£119.00	£58.00	5	12	4	8
13	17" TFT Mitsubisi	monitor	23/03/2003	£299.00	£149.00	2	5	7	8
14	P4 2.5GHz	computer	30/03/2003	£999.00	£599.00	3	8	5	7
15	L&G 56k	modem	01/04/2003	£59.00	£29.00	5	5	5	11

A printout of my complete database after I updated it

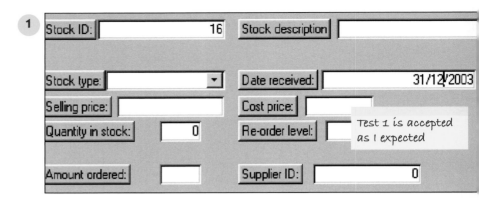

Test 1 is accepted as I expected

Test 1 has shown that the extreme data that I entered has been accepted by the system as I expected.

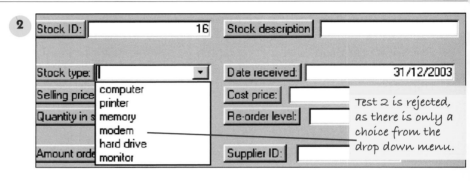

Test 2 is rejected, as there is only a choice from the drop down menu.

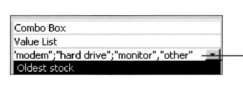

Test 2 has shown up a problem with my database. There is no way of adding a stock type that I haven't already stocked. I will change the menu and add other. I have shown it here.

Test 3 prevents invalid data being entered to my Stock table. I thought it was a good idea to use validation rules, especially as I could decide the error message. I felt that this message was clear to the user.

4

Stock ID	Stock description	Stock type	Date received
5	HP Deskjet 90	printer	02/05/2003
2	P4 2.0GHz	computer	02/05/2003
1	P4 1.8GHz	computer	23/04/2003
15	L&G 56k	modem	01/04/2003
14	P4 2.5GHz	computer	30/03/2003
13	17"		23/03/2003
4	Eps		23/03/2003
12	Max		22/03/2003
11	15"		21/03/2003
10	19"		20/03/2003
9	Max		15/03/2003
8	256Kb RAM	memory	12/03/2003
7	128Kb RAM	memory	12/03/2003
6	Canon 340C	printer	10/03/2003
3	P4 2.3GHz	computer	10/03/2003

Test 4 has produced the same set of results as I expected. I simply changed my sort to Descending to get the most recent first.

Test 4 has worked as I expected. I am pleased that I only did one of these tests as my teacher said it was only a simple test.

5

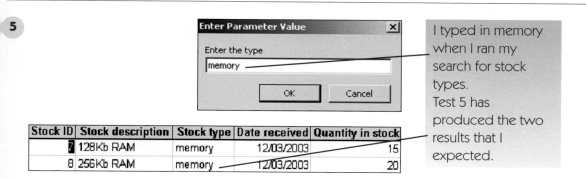

Enter Parameter Value

Enter the type

`memory`

| OK | Cancel |

Stock ID	Stock description	Stock type	Date received	Quantity in stock
7	128Kb RAM	memory	12/03/2003	15
8	256Kb RAM	memory	12/03/2003	20

I typed in memory when I ran my search for stock types.
Test 5 has produced the two results that I expected.

6

Stock ID	Stock description	Stock type	Cost price	Quantity	Re-order	Amount	Company name	Address1	Address2
2	P4 2.0GHz	computer	£359.00	1	3	8	Fresniere Computers	22 Cromwell Road	Bramley
11	15" TFT Mitsubisi	monitor	£129.00	2	3	5	Wong Supplies	43 Sandwich Road	Sheffield
12	Maxtor 120Gb HD	hard drive	£58.00	4	5	12	Wong Supplies	43 Sandwich Road	Sheffield

Test 6 went according to my plan. After the database had been updated, I ran the search. It found the three items of stock which were under-stocked and linked them to the Suppliers table.

Coursework Adviser's comment

Good Points
- As stated earlier, Rachel has set up a partial test plan, which is necessary for the award of more than half marks.
- This has been followed, and Rachel did well to pick up a weakness in the design, which didn't allow for other types of stock to be entered.

Areas for Improvement
- Only a limited set of tests of specific cases for the Stock table have taken place. There is no testing of the Suppliers table and only one test of the links between the tables.
- It would be expected that the mail merge would be tested.

Testing a spreadsheet sub-problem

- It is essential that you test all the sections of your project for which you have to enter data regularly – a spreadsheet.

- Spreadsheet tests can focus on the **data-entry stage** (validation of data) and the **correctness of formulae** used.

- The test should also show that any **data links** are correctly implemented.

4.49 *Extract from Rachel's spreadsheet testing stage showing a different method of testing*

Spreadsheet test plan 1
<u>What to test?</u>
I will test that the formula for the gross pay works –
hours worked × rate of pay
<u>How to test it?</u>
I will select two employees and test that their gross pay
is correct by working out hours (worked) × rate per hour
<u>Test data to use</u>
Alan – 8 hours and £3.50 per hour
Sue – 20 hours and £7.50 per hour

<u>Expected results</u>
Alan Memory   £3.50 × 8   = **£28.00**
Sue Simms   £7.50 × 12   = **£90.00**

Wages	First name	Last name	hours	per hour	Gross pay	
	Jane	Byte	£ 12.00	35	£ 420.00	
	Dave	Ramm	£ 9.50	30	£ 285.00	
	Alan	Memory	£ 3.50	8	£ 28.00	
	Sue	Simms	£ 7.50	12	£ 90.00	
					£ 823.00	

My printout of part of the spreadsheet shows the Gross pay. Alan and Sue's pay is the same as I expected, so I think my formula works correctly.

Coursework Adviser's comments

Good Points

- Rachel has produced a further section from a test plan. This has been followed, and she has commented on the results.

Areas for Improvement

- There is only one specific test case for this spreadsheet. This aspect alone is insufficient to gain many marks. Other types of formula should be tested as well.
- There are no validation rules tested.
- The search to export the correct data from the database to the spreadsheet would need to be tested.

UNIT 5: EVALUATION

SESSION 1 ▬ Evaluating a publishing solution

■ From your Analysis, copy and paste the **desired outcomes** and **performance criteria** relating to the sub-problem that you are going to evaluate. Remember to take into account any **changes** made between the Design and Implementation stages.

4.50 *Extract from Rachel's evaluation of her poster*

Performance criteria and desired outcomes for shop poster

The poster will contain all required details.
- It will be printed in colour on A4 paper in portrait.
- The top two-thirds will always be the same.
- The bottom third will change.
- The poster will be reusable because a template of the fixed items on the poster will be saved with an empty frame in the bottom part.
- It will be saved as 'Poster template'.

I checked that I had included all the required details on the poster. My poster contains the title and logo at the top. I grouped them together so that it made it easy to move them around. This also helped me when I copied and pasted them into the other adverts (letter-headed paper and website), as they were much easier to make the correct size for each one. Using a text box to contain the opening hours was efficient, as again it provided me with more control over the

movement of the text on the page. I used the same technique for the company and website addresses, but removed the border around the frame, as it looked more effective underneath the shop name and logo. I kept the same font name for each section, as it would have looked unprofessional if I'd kept changing it.

I made reasonably conservative use of colour, but it was effective because the colour scheme was consistent for the shop name and special offers – the yellows and greys matched well with computer equipment which could be bought at the shop.

My poster, with the blank special-offers section, was saved as **poster template** in my GCSE ICT folder – I changed its properties to Read Only so I couldn't accidentally save over it when I later added special offers.

Coursework Adviser's comments
Good Points
- *Rachel has discussed the effectiveness of parts of the solution by referring to ways in which it has been efficiently produced, thus achieving a high mark for this section.*

Areas for Improvement
- *Rachel should comment on all the performance criteria – there is no reference to the change in division of the page from two-thirds/one-third into two halves.*
- *Rachel has not evaluated the whole solution at this stage.*

Evaluating a database solution

4.51 *Extract from Rachel's evaluation of her database*

- Each sub-problem should be evaluated **independently**.
- Provide an **overall evaluation** of the whole project when complete.

Performance criteria and desired outcomes for stock and supplier database

- A stock table with essential details (ID, type, description, date, cost and selling price, re-order level, amount ordered, quantity and supplier code)
- A supplier table with essential details (supplier code, name, address, postcode)
- A way of showing all stock of a certain type
- A way of showing under-stocked items
- A way of linking the tables so that orders could be placed for the correct items and sent to the correct supplier
- A way of re-ordering under-stocked items

I checked that I had included the essential fields for the **Stock table**. I made minor changes to the field names for convenience and rearranged some fields, e.g. I put the **Description** field before the **Type**. I added a field called **Sold**, so I could check what stock had been sold each day. This made it simple to transfer data to my spreadsheet. I didn't think of this in my analysis, as I didn't realise how complicated it would be to transfer each item of stock sold individually. I also validated the **Sold** field to be greater than 0 and included a validation message. This was to prevent entering a negative amount accidentally, if I thought it was being taken away from the **Quantity in stock**.

The main fields for the **Suppliers table** remained the same. I decided to split the **address** field into two for convenience when doing the mail-merge letter.

This made it quicker to enter and more accurate. I would have had to repeat the supplier details several times for different items of stock otherwise.

When searched for stock of a certain type, I made the field into a **drop-down menu** to make data entry very quick. I sorted out a design fault where I hadn't catered for other types of stock to be entered. It was much easier to set up a search for stock type than I thought, as I used a **parameter search**. This meant I didn't have to change the search each time, I just had to type in the stock type as I used it.

My search for under-stocked items worked well. I checked if the **Re-order level** was greater than the **Quantity in stock**. I printed out all these records and linked them to the Suppliers table.

Linking the tables together was simple. I called the link field by the same name and dragged it from one table to the other to establish the link. Next I chose to include the fields from each table that I needed by selecting them in my query called **Re-orders**.

I used the letter-headed paper that I'd produced in the publishing section to set up a mail-merge letter. It had the supplier address detail from the **Suppliers** table and the stock details from the **Stock** table. I used the mail merge with my search for under-stocked items. This part of my database was the most useful, as I could check for under-stocked items in my database before using the letter head and the mail-merge letter to suppliers.

Coursework Adviser's comments

Good Points

- Rachel has clearly discussed the **effectiveness** of the solution by referring to ways in which it has been produced.
- **Efficiency** is implied in the commentary. A high mark would be given for this section.

Areas for Improvement

- Rachel should explain more clearly why changes have been made to the original analysis.
- To achieve maximum marks, Rachel should make an **overall evaluation** of the solution.

SESSION 1 — Producing a user guide

⇨ Create a separate booklet for the User Guide

- Start your user guide with a **contents page**. Only include activities which are going to be reused on a regular basis.
- Put different activities in **separate sections**.
- Make the activities clear by including **screen shots** to display what is happening.
- Make sure you consider the **end user** who may have to carry out the tasks if the regular user if absent from work.

MARK ALLOCATION

The maximum mark you can be awarded for your User Guide is 10.

Contents

Poster
(a) Changing the special offers — Page 1
Web pages
(a) Changing the new stock page — Page 2
Stock table
(a) Adding new stock — Page 3
(b) Changing stock details — Page 3
(c) Finding specific types of stock — Page 3
(d) Re-ordering under-stocked items — Page 4
Profit/loss spreadsheet
(a) Setting up next week's spreadsheet — Page 5

4.52 *Extract from Rachel's User Guide – Contents page*

HINTS

- Note that Rachel hasn't included her User Guide sections for the poster and webpages.
- She only needs to explain how to enter data for the Special Offers section of the poster and the new stock page of the website, as these are the areas that relate to reuse.

4.53 *Extract from Rachel's User Guide – showing the database reuse on page 3*

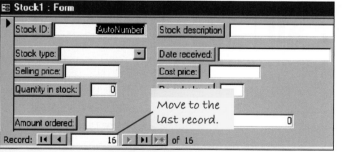

Adding new stock
Page 3 (a)
Open the database called **Stock** and choose the form called **Stock1**. Type in the details for the new stock item. The Stock ID will be generated automatically. Choose the Stock type from the drop-down menu. Save the database after changes and back up the data.

Changing stock details
Page 3 (b)
'Bytes for all' has sold three of the P4 2.3GHz computers at £579 each. Choose the form **Stock1** and move to the correct record using the forward arrows. Reduce the Quantity in stock by three and save the database.

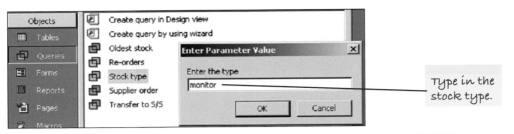

Finding specific types of stock
Page 3 (c)
Choose the search called **Stock type**, enter the type you want. Print it out to show the bank manager.

Stock ID	Stock description	Stock type	Date received	Selling price	Quantity
10	19" Monitor liama	monitor	20/03/2003	£225.00	8
11	15" TFT Mitsubisi	monitor	21/03/2003	£259.00	2
13	17" TFT Mitsubisi	monitor	23/03/2003	£299.00	7

Re-ordering under-stocked items

Page 4 (d)
1 Delete the items sold for the previous day.
2 Enter the new items sold.
3 Reduce the **Quantity in stock** by the same amount.
4 Choose the query called **Re-orders**.
5 Open the mail merge called **Mail-merge letter**:
6 Check the query and print it before using the mail merge called **Mail-merge letter** to re-order any under-stocked items from the correct supplier.

4.54 *Extract from Rachel's User Guide – showing the database reuse on page 4*

	Create query in Design view
	Create query by using wizard
	Oldest stock
	Re-orders
	Stock type
	Supplier order
	Transfer to S/S

ID	Stock description	Stock type	Cost price	Quantity	Re-order	Amount	Company name	Address1	Address2	Post Code
1	P4 2.0GHz	computer	£359.00	1	3	8	Fresniere Computers	22 Cromwell Road	Bramley	BR7 6TL
11	15" TFT Mitsubisi	monitor	£129.00	2	3	5	Wong Supplies	43 Sandwich Road	Sheffield	S13 1EE
12	Maxtor 120Gb HD	hard drive	£58.00	4	5	12	Wong Supplies	43 Sandwich Road	Sheffield	S13 1EE

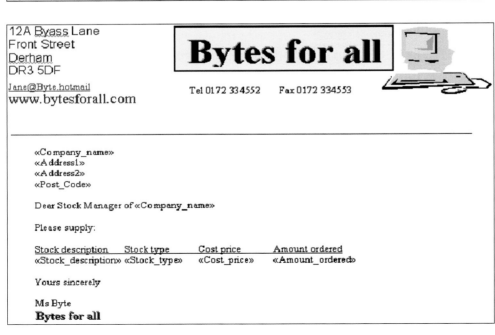

After checking the suppliers of the under-stocked items, open the mail-merge letter and run the **mail merge**. Print out a letter for each supplier and send it in the post. Include today's date in the file name when saving the merged letters, then Exit.

Setting up next week's spreadsheet

Page 5 (a)

Open the spreadsheet called **sales&payments**

2 Copy a blank spreadsheet template into next week's worksheet.

3 In the **Stock** database, run the search for sales this week called **Transfer to S/S**

4 Copy all the records across to the spreadsheet to cell **A5**.

5 Enter the hours for the employees in cells **D16 to D19**.

6 Print a copy for me.

7 Save the spreadsheet with today's date added to the file name.

4.55 *Extract from Rachel's User Guide – showing the spreadsheet reuse on page 5*

	A	B	C	D	E	F	G	H	
1	Bytes for all: sales and Payments spreadsheet								
2	Sales this week		23/05/2003						
3							start balance -£		184.00
4	Stock ID	Stock description	Stock type	Date received	Selling price	Cost price	Sold	Total	
5								£	-
6								£	-
7								£	-
8								£	-
9							TOTAL	£	184.00
10	Payments								
11								per week	
12	Electricity							£	52.00
13	Rent							£	250.00
14	Rates							£	135.00
15	Wages	First name	Last name	hours	per hour	Gross pay			
16		Jane	Byte		£ 12.00	£ -			
17		Dave	Ramm		£ 9.50	£ -			
18		Alan	Memory		£ 3.50	£ -			
19		Sue	Simms		£ 7.50	£ -			
20								£	-
21						TOTAL		£	437.00
22									
23						PROFIT		-£	621.00

Coursework Adviser's comments

Good Points

- Rachel has separated the guide into sections and made it clear and easy to use.
- The step-by-step use, in non-technical language, adopted is entirely appropriate for this section.
- Spelling, punctuation and grammar are consistently accurate.

Areas for Improvement

- From the evidence of the contents page, Rachel hasn't produced a complete guide. For example, when using the Stock table, she hasn't included advice about all routines needed (e.g. displaying items of stock in order of data received).
- There is no advice about how to change data in the Suppliers table.

CHECK YOURSELF ANSWERS AND COMMENTS

SECTION 1
UNIT 1 INPUT DEVICES

1 Types of input devices (page 3)

Q1 Mouse and keyboard

COMMENTS The mouse and keyboard are the most commonly used input devices because much of our data is entered on a keyboard, and most user-computer activity is 'point and click' via the mouse.

Q2 Microphone and midi Instruments

COMMENT Sound of any sort can be captured using a microphone, but only musical data is captured using midi.

Q3 Scanner, digital camera, video digitiser

COMMENT Although images can be drawn on a graphics tablet, existing images can only be captured using the three devices given.

2 Other ways of capturing data (page 5)

Q1 Fast, efficient input of data

COMMENT Remember that supermarkets have bar-code readers, scanning the codes on products. Imagine the chaos if this system broke down – long queues!

Q2 OMRs read pencil marks from specially prepared boxes on paper; OCRs read proper characters as a picture which software converts to text.

COMMENT Pencil marks can represent a character if it is in a certain position on a form, but it is quite different to recognise a character written anywhere on a page.

Q3 Banks

COMMENT Equipment for MICR is very expensive and so generally only banks have invested in this type of data-capture method.

UNIT 2 OUTPUT DEVICES

1 Common output devices (page 7)

Q1 Displaying output to the computer user

COMMENTS Monitors are used for displaying output to the user. Just because we select items on the screen does not make it an input device. Touch screens display output and can also accept input, but these are special devices.

Q2 Dot matrix

Q3 Laser

COMMENTS Dot matrix is the noisiest and cheapest printer (and so is least common these days) whilst the laser is the quietest and fastest .

Q4 Presentations

COMMENTS Speakers can be used for listening to sound in a multimedia presentation. Multimedia is when sound, text, pictures and video are used.

2 Other output devices (page 8)

Q1 They are more accurate and flexible because pens are used.

COMMENT Remember that plotters draw lines exactly where they are required using precisely positiond pens.

Q2 Robot arm

COMMENT Greenhouse windows, car-park barriers – in fact, anything that opens, closes or rotates involves a motor in a computerised control system.

UNIT 3 COMPUTER SYSTEMS HARDWARE

I Inside the computer (page 9)

QI Central processing unit – does all the processing.

COMMENT The CPU has two main items present (the control unit and the arithmetic and logic unit); you may wish to include descriptions of these two items in your answer.

Q2 Internal: small in size, stores current instructions and data
Backing storage: large and stores all programs and data

COMMENT Internal memory is only about 256–512 MB in a typical home computer, whilst hard-disk size is measured in gigabytes (1GB = 1,000 MB)

Q3 Hard disk, floppy disk

COMMENT Other common examples are CD-Rs, zip drives and CD-RWs.

2 Different types of computer (page 11)

QI A laptop is smaller and portable. It is also more robust (not easily broken).

COMMENT Other factors are the type of monitor (LCD for laptop) and cost (laptop more expensive for same processing power).

Q2 A supercomputer

COMMENTS These machines are really confined to being used by government organisations or similar massive operations. The mainframe is used by large-scale businesses.

UNIT 4 STORAGE

I Internal memory (page 12)

QI Random Access Memory – it stores current items you are working on.

COMMENT 'Current items' are the data and instruction currently being executed by the computer.

Q2 ROM makes sure that the computer system starts up properly.

COMMENT 'The contents of ROM cannot be destroyed for this reason.

2 Backing storage (page 14)

QI Floppy disk and magnetic tape

COMMENT 'Hard disks are not usually portable unless they are mounted in special removable hard-disk drives.

Q2 CD-RW is used to write to as well as read from, whereas a CD-ROM can only be read.

COMMENT Do not confuse internal ROM with CD-ROMs, but remember both are read-only memory.

Q3 Hard disk and CD-RW

COMMENTS The database will need to be updated, so it must be possible to regularly write to the item. It must also be of sufficient size. Tape would not be appropriate, as we do not want to read all items when we only may want to search for one item of data.

UNIT 5 LINKING COMPUTERS TOGETHER

I Computers communicating (page 15)

QI A computer that is connected to one or more computers

COMMENT Remember that a network card is a very important piece of hardware for a computer that needs to communicate and exchange data with other computers.

Q2 When computers are located a long way from each other

COMMENT Satellites are used for very long-distance data transmission across continents.

Q3 Wire and fibre optic

COMMENT Remember that fibre-optic cable uses light, and wire uses electrical pulses to transmit the data.

2 Networks (page 17)

Q1 Sharing and communication

COMMENT If you can remember these two words, it is easy to think about the sort of things it is possible to share, such as data, printers and software.

Q2 Star, Ring and Bus

COMMENT Think about cable layout when you identify the topologies.

Q3 a) Local Area Network
b) Wide Area Network
c) Geographic area

COMMENTS Remember that 'AN' stands for Area Network. Think about the factor of geographical location of computers. If they are collected in a small geographic area, that means they are in the same locality, so it should help you remember 'L' stands for Local. If they are located over a wide area, then the 'W' stands for Wide.

UNIT 6 LEGAL ISSUES

1 Copyright and misuse (page 18)

Q1 A legal document that covers all computers that are networked within an organisation to use a particular piece of software.

COMMENT Because software is expensive to write, companies want to be sure that people who want to use their software have paid for it. A licence is one way of doing this.

Q2 Attempting to break into a computer or a computer users' network area to look at, change, delete or steal data.

COMMENTS Hacking is often achieved by guessing user-IDs and passwords. Once access has been gained, the hacker can do what they want with data and programs.

Q3 Deliberately spreading viruses, electronic fraud

COMMENT Remember that software piracy is also covered.

2 Data Protection Act (page 20)

Q1 1984 and 1998

COMMENT It is important to remember these two dates.

Q2 The Data Controller is the person in the organisation who controls the collection, processing and release of data, and the DPC is the person who is notified of and regulates organisations' activities according to the details of the notification.

COMMENT The Data Controller works within the organisation. The DPC is external and regulates practice in all organisations according to the Act.

Q3 Data must be: processed fairly and lawfully; held and processed for registered purpose(s); relevant and not excessive to the purpose; kept safe and secure; kept accurate and up to date; kept no longer than necessary; processed according to the rights of the data subject; kept within the EU.

COMMENT These short phrases will help you remember all eight principles.

Q4 Tax records; crime records; domestic records; national security records; artistic, literary, historical, statistical or research data; and data which is held in order to regulate membership.

COMMENT Again, it is important to remember these exemptions.

Unit 7 Social issues

1 Computers in everyday life (page 21)

Q1 It's fast to get through tills due to speedy scanning of bar codes and also we get an itemised bill to show what we have bought and how much each item costs.

COMMENT These are also similar advantages to shopping in many large department stores

Q2 Bank account information could be intercepted by a hacker and used later for themselves. Also, it may be that we buy something we don't like when we eventually get to see it.

COMMENT Additionally, you would be correct to say that you may inadvertently access undesirable material whilst browsing the Internet, but the two reasons given are more appropriate answers.

2 Computers at work (page 22)

Q1 Clerical and manual workers

COMMENT These are the two main areas where redundancies have been noted, due to computers being good at filing and doing repetitive tasks.

Q2 Secretary

COMMENT Remember, you could also give any design-based job, such as an architect.

Q3 Reduced costs of accommodation

COMMENT This is the most obvious answer. Many running costs associated with the accommodation, such as light and heat, are also reduced.

Unit 8 Health and safety

1 Computers, health and safety (page 23)

Q1 a) Repetitive Strain Injury and eyestrain

b) RSI can be prevented by using a wrist support and also by taking regular breaks. Eyestrain can be prevented by installing diffused overhead lighting to avoid glare and also by installing window blinds.

COMMENTS These are the two main health problems, which are more related to using the computer rather than the way we sit, as with back problems or doing any work for a long time which could cause stress

Remember to relate each prevention method correctly. If you have chosen back problems or backache in part a), you should talk about a height-adjustable chair, not a comfortable chair.

Q2 Trailing wires should be avoided to ensure no one trips over them and suffers an injury. Fire extinguishers should be installed to prevent spread of fire, should one occur.

COMMENT Remember to write in full sentences when you are asked to describe, illustrating your depth of knowledge.

2 Keeping data safe (page 25)

Q1 A backup is a copy of data (or even a program) currently in use. Its purpose is to ensure that it is possible to recover data if the main copy is lost.

COMMENT This is a fairly common question with a straightforward answer

Q2 Virus protection software could be used to clean off the virus.

COMMENT It is unusual to find a different method to do this, but sometimes there are special steps involving the location and deletion of files. Your answer should focus on virus detection and disinfecting using the software.

Q3 Encryption which uses rules or a code to convert data to an unreadable format, and user-IDs and passwords which are used to identify the user and make sure who they say they are.

COMMENTS The other answer you could give would be to describe physical locks. It is important that you show that your answer indicates that you understand what encryption is and what user-IDs and passwords are. Do not confuse encryption with encoding/coding data. Coding data merely abbreviates data stored in records using a particular format to reduce data entry time and the amount of space that it takes up.

UNIT 9 DIFFERENT TYPES OF PROCESSING

1 Batch processing (page 27)

Q1 Visual check and double-entry verification. Validation checks are: range check and check-digit check.

COMMENTS Visual checks can be done when there is a small volume of data (not usual for batch systems), whilst double entry is when two operators key the same data in, and the system warns the second operator if there is an error to investigate. Other checks, such as picture check and field-length checks, are also common answers.

Q2 Large volumes of data are processed at set periods, and the master file does not have to be up to date all the time.

COMMENT These are two main characteristics, and you should be familiar with them.

Q3 Sorting of transactions

COMMENTS You should know this step. Being able to explain why it is necessary would score high marks, although in this case it is not necessary, as you are only asked to name the step.

2 Online/Real-time processing (page 28)

Q1 Because it is important to process incoming data immediately so that the computer can respond and control the environment in which the system operates.

COMMENTS Think about being able to control the temperature in a greenhouse. If it gets too hot, the windows need to be opened immediately, hence a real-time system is necessary.

Q2 Always up to date and immediate output produced

COMMENT These are two main characteristics, and you should be familiar with them.

Q3 a) real time   b) batch   c) online

COMMENTS The first two examples are more obvious. The third example is likely to fool you, but booking systems often operate as an online system because it is impossible to provide real-time access to all the travel agents accessing the information. Instead, the bookings get updated when the travel agents close.

UNIT 10 SYSTEMS CYCLE

1 Steps of the systems cycle (page 29)

Q1 Analysis, Design, Development and testing, Implementation

COMMENT This requires you to learn the steps in order

Q2 Collecting documents such as orders, interviewing order processing clerks

COMMENT This type of question will require reference to the context, in this case order processing. Do not just ignore the context in your answer.

Q3 Direct and parallel

COMMENT The most contrasting methods are direct and parallel, because with parallel running, both old and new systems run together, whilst with direct, the old system goes as the new one starts to be used.

2 Systems analysis (page 30)

Q1 It focuses the investigation around the data which is processed; this then makes it easier to identify how the data is currently processed and stored.

COMMENTS Remember that the two things that make up a system are data and processes. Input data is processed, stored and then processed again to produce output. As soon as data documents (input or stored items) are identified, it provides a starting point for asking about what happens in the current system.

Q2 Without identifying user needs, a new system may provide unnecessary information.

COMMENTS *Users do not always want what the system designer thinks they need. The system designer should not waste time on features that the user does not need.*

3 Systems design, development, testing and implementation (page 32)

Q1 Purchase hardware and software, develop system and test, train users, user testing, install system onto purchased hardware

COMMENT *Many of these items are based on sound background knowledge, but you will also need to use your common sense.*

Q2 Data structures, screens, reports, enter test data, testing, user testing

COMMENTS *Note that users cannot test the system until the system is error free. Also, screen inputs and outputs cannot be set up until the basic data structures to hold data are in place.*

Q3 Consistent layout, clear instructions

COMMENTS *These two features are the basic knowledge needed to answer this type of question, but if you are asked to design an input form, you will need to think about other items, such as ensuring there is a clear title, sensible colour scheme, logical layout, maybe even tick boxes for certain items.*

UNIT 11 SYSTEMS SOFTWARE

1 Operating systems and user interface software (page 33)

Q1 An operating system schedules tasks and organises memory.

COMMENT *These are the two main tasks, but remember the operating system also has to respond to user commands, transfer data and do many other things. At GCSE, you do not need to know too much detail.*

Q2 Two GUI features: there are icons to click on; there are menus to select from.

COMMENT *The answer is hidden in the features of a WIMP environment (i.e. windows, icons, menus, pointers). Remember, a WIMP environment is the same as a GUI.*

2 Translators and utilities (page 34)

Q1 It converts programing language instruction into machine code. Machine code is the binary code that the computer understands.

COMMENT *This answer is a full answer, indicating not only an understanding of what a translator does, but also that machine code is equivalent to binary code.*

Q2 Utility software is systems software which allows tasks to be carried out to keep your computer system running. Virus-checking software checks your system for viruses and can also disinfect viruses, helping to keep the system working.

COMMENTS *This question asks for a two-part answer. Try and make sure you spot this type of question and aim to achieve maximum marks with an answer that links the two elements of the question.*

UNIT 12 BUSINESS APPLICATIONS SOFTWARE

1 Word processors and desktop publishers (page 36)

Q1 essay (A), thesis (A), poster (B), birthday card (B), memo (A), advertising booklet (B)

COMMENTS *This type of question will probably also include other items of software and tasks to match up, so could potentially be more difficult. The most difficult item to decide upon is the advertising booklet, which could be just text. This is unlikely, as special layout and colourful objects will often be included for advertising materials.*

Q2 A text frame would be created, then the text would be imported; a picture frame would be created for the digital photograph to be imported (or Insert picture from File could be used); the results could be copied from the spreadsheet and pasted into place or imported into place. Each item would be moved around until the right layout was achieved. A title could be created and perhaps rotated at an angle for effect. A coloured background and border could be used.

COMMENTS There will be a range of marks for all sorts of actions you could include. There are also many ways of achieving the results. You should focus on getting the three items placed in the document and making a point about the layout.

2 Spreadsheets (page 37)

Q1 =(C1+D1)*100

COMMENTS Learn how to write down formulae and make sure you know = is the first thing you should write down.

Q2 Highlight cell C3, go to the Edit menu and select Copy, then highlight cells C4 to C20, go to the Edit menu and click on Paste.

COMMENTS You must state the cell references that are used in your answer, remembering not to highlight the cell you are copying from before you do the paste. This answer is a stock answer and should be memorised, although there are alternative and quicker ways to replicate cells.

Q3 Having formulae which recalculate when data in cells are changed. Being able to answer 'what if' questions.

COMMENTS These are two similar, but clear advantages. You could also mention how easy it is to replicate, which means that there is no danger of mistyping formulae.

3 Databases (page 39)

Q1 Decide on which fields are required, decide on the data types, set the field lengths, set up a key field, set up any validation rules and save the data structure/table.

COMMENTS Notice in the answer that there is no mention of entering data. You could say that the data structure is now ready to accept data. As the question only asks for design of the database, you could stop at this point. Look at the number of marks allocated to the question; if you only have three or four marks, this answer should be sufficient. Sometimes this question will appear as a jumbled list you have to order, rather than you thinking up all the items yourself.

Q2 Car type=saloon AND colour=black OR colour=white

COMMENTS The key to this type of answer is to think about different fields and use AND when you have two fields or use OR when you have the same field. If we had asked for AND with the colour field only, cars that were painted both black and white (two-tone cars) could appear on the output list.

4 Computer-Aided Design (page 40)

Q1 Items can be drawn or selected from a library of objects, and designs can be shown in three-dimensions, allowing different views to be seen.

COMMENTS Different design packages have different features, but most will show three-dimensional images and also different views. Many have a library of objects or the facility to create a library of objects.

Q2 The architect can draw accurately to scale, easily editing work rather than having to draw and redraw items from scratch.

COMMENTS The biggest labour-saving feature of these packages is the fact that manually drawing every single item is not necessary and changes are much easier.

5 The Internet and e-mail (page 42)

Q1 A modem and telephone line, a browser and dial-up software to access an ISP

COMMENTS You could also say an ISDN line instead of modem and telephone line. If you choose a modem, remember to include a standard telephone line in your answer as well. One will not work without the other. Dial-up software gives you access via the communication line to your ISP. You will need the telephone number of your ISP.

Q2 Attaching files and forwarding mail

COMMENTS There are many features of e-mail. The best way to revise this topic is to check your e-mail system and see what is on offer. Try to remember three distinct features and use them regularly before the examination.

UNIT 13 DATA LOGGING AND CONTROL

1 Data logging (page 43)

Q1 Light sensors could detect when a beam is broken. The beam would be directed at the light sensor across the doorway. Each time the beam is broken, someone will have entered the store. This could increment a count. Different time intervals could be set, and then the count would start again. Data would be stored for each period, until a set of figures was gathered for an entire week. Alternatively, a pressure pad could be used so that when someone steps on it, a count is incremented.

COMMENTS Make yourself aware of different sensors and how they could be used. This will help you identify more than one sensor in a question like this

Q2 Advantages: operates 24 hours, taking readings at regular intervals; it is accurate and consistent about taking readings.

COMMENTS Two distinct and clear advantages. If you can memorise them so as to avoid the common answer of 'never needs a break'.

2 Control systems (page 44)

Q1 A humidity sensor, a temperature sensor

To maintain constant temperature, the temperature readings taken by the sensor are compared with the constant value. If the temperature reading is higher than the required constant value, a motor could open the windows or, if heaters are on, switch the heaters off. If the temperature reading is lower, windows will close and heaters may be switched on.

COMMENTS Knowing inputs, processing and outputs for a few common examples of control systems will help with this type of question. Remember, there is always some comparison made to set values to cause the output to happen.

UNIT 14 APPLICATIONS

1 Multimedia systems (page 45)

Q1 Information can be presented in a variety of different ways. It is also much more compact than the book version.

COMMENTS Although the question doesn't ask for advantages compared to conventional encyclopaedias in book version, this is implied in the question.

Q2 Sound, Animation

COMMENTS Pick answers that clearly show that you know there are other media than the text and graphics you would find in printed copies.

2 Applications in the home (page 47)

Q1 PIR to detect movement inside a room. Contact switches which, when a window opens, break the circuit and set off the alarm.

COMMENTS This type of question is related to theory about control systems and sensors. An alternative sensor might be a pressure pad in a doorway to detect when someone enters the room. The two sensors in the answer are the most common.

Q2 User input is selection of a washing programme using a keypad or buttons. There will be a display of some sort to indicate the programme selected and its current state. The programme is initiated and controls the switching on and off of the heater, pump and water input. Sensors will detect water temperature and volume of water inside the machine. This also governs the actions of the processor.

COMMENTS Your answer should discuss user input, input from sensors, processing and output.

3 Business applications (page 49)

Q1 When the book is scanned, the loans file is searched for a match on the book code. The loan record for that book is then deleted, so that the member details are no longer associated with the book.

COMMENTS Stock control, supermarkets, bar codes and order processing are key areas that are linked together.

Q2 Till receipt

COMMENT There is only one answer to this question. It is easy to remember if you are clear about how any EPOS works.

4 Expert systems (page 50)

Q1 A knowledgebase of facts and rules, an inference engine and a question answer style interface is used to provide expert advice or a diagnosis. The user types in a query or problem, and the system will ask a series of questions. Using information that the user supplies to answers, the inference engine looks for matched rules and facts, so that conclusions can be drawn. Advice or a diagnosis can then be displayed. The user can even ask the expert system why it came to the conclusion it did.

COMMENTS Stating components before explaining how the system works is a good strategy. It makes the answer clear.

Q2 Interview experts, design an interface and specify how the inference engine will work.
Design a knowledgebase, and develop the system.
Test the system with experts and then implement and evaluate it.

COMMENTS Think about the system cycle and apply it to this type of system. It is then easier to remember the steps to be taken.

UNIT 15 EXAM PRACTICE

Answers to Questions to try (short course)

Q1 a) There is a large quantity of data to choose from which is always up to date. (1 mark)

b) CD-ROMs are easy to search because with one key word you get all the relevant data. There are no irrelevant sites displayed, as you would find on the Internet. (1 mark)

COMMENT You would gain 1 mark for part (a). For part (b), you could also say that there is no need to subscribe to an Internet Service Provider or go online when using a CD-ROM.

Q2 An e-mail link (1), so that the person browsing the website can make contact (1), button or hyperlink (1) to another part of the website or to a different website (1). Graphics or moving images (1) could be included to help focus the viewer's attention (1).

COMMENT There is 1 mark for identifying a feature and 1 mark for saying how it is used. Any two of these items with a good reason each will gain full marks. A hot spot could also have been included.

Q3 a) A virus is a computer program (1), which spreads from program to program, usually causing problems as it spreads (1).

b) To help prevent getting a virus, you can install anti-virus software (1) or make sure you do not download viruses from the Internet when opening e-mail or browsing the Web (1).

COMMENT In part (a), the second mark is awarded for stating the virus causes problems. However, if you just said the virus spreads you would also get the second mark. In part (b), there is 1 mark for each valid way you can prevent getting a virus. Stating that you do not allow Internet access would not be valid, but you could say that you will not let anyone use floppy disks in your machine without first virus checking.

Q4 a) Anemometer (measures wind speed) (1), temperature sensor measures temperature (1)

b) The data is analogue data and has to be converted to digital format before it can be recorded on the computer (1). To do this, an analogue-to-digital converter (ADC) is used (1)

c) To monitor weather patterns and forecast the weather (1)

COMMENT *The spread of marks for each point is shown in brackets within the answer.*

Q5 One way: Computers could be used for fraud. Hackers could obtain credit card or bank details and use them to buy goods or obtain cash (1).

Second way: A person's data could be used for a reason that it shouldn't, breaking the Data Protection Act (1).

Third way: Software could be used without purchasing a licence, breaking the Software Copyright and Patents law (1).

COMMENT *Another answer could be: Hackers can look, change or delete data which they do not have authorisation to do. This could be used to replace the first part of the answer above. Try to mention three separate laws Computer Misuse, Data Protection and Copyright.*

Q6 First safety hazard: Trailing wires could cause tripping (1).

Second safety hazard: Electrical hazard could be caused unless separate sockets are used for plugs (1).

COMMENT *Remember to target safety, not health hazards.*

Q7 Discussion of the following points (each point gets one mark):

• No need to leave home.
• Good for the disabled or homebound, or for those working shifts or awkward hours.
• Lots of choice, as there are many sites and products advertised on the Internet.
• Some products that are unavailable in shops in this country are available over the Internet.

• Cannot try or see products in real life, and they may not be what you imagined.
• Need a credit card to buy items.
• Sites may not be secure, so credit-card details cannot always be transmitted safely.
• Some people prefer to go out shopping, as they see other people and often other products they were not necessarily looking for. This makes the shopping experience more pleasurable for some.

COMMENT *Try and balance the number of advantages and disadvantages you discuss; although there may be allowance in the mark scheme for imbalance, you will still have to think of both advantages and disadvantages. Here, there are four advantages and four disadvantages, so a good balance is achieved.*

Answers to Questions to try (full course)

Q1 Verifying data is when a check is made to ensure that the data which is recorded on the computer is exactly the same as the data on the source document (1). Validating data is when a number of checks are applied to ensure that the data input is reasonable (1).

COMMENT *One mark is awarded for stating clearly what verification is and one mark for validation.*

Q2 c and e (2)

COMMENT *A good tip for identifying real-time systems is to think about whether the processing can wait. In these two systems, clearly they would not be able to operate without continuous and immediate processing.*

Q3 Any two of the following choices for 2 marks: pilot, phased, direct, parallel, with the corresponding advantages for a further 2 marks:

Pilot: Small area can be thoroughly checked for any problems before full implementation.

Phased: Each area changes over to the new system step by step, so it is easier to mange for the technical staff.

Direct: Old system goes and new system is put straight in, so there is an immediate benefit.

Parallel: Both old and new system run together, so staff have time to get used to the system.

COMMENT It doesn't matter which two of these four you choose, but you will get one mark for identifying the method and one mark for stating the advantage.

Q4 A standard letter is created using a word processor (1). A data source is created with the names and addresses of customers (1). The data source is linked to the standard letter (1). Merge fields are inserted from the linked data source (1). The letter is merged to create personalized letters (1).

COMMENT There are five points made in this answer, with the mark shown in brackets after each point made. You only need to write about four of these points to get the 4 marks available.

Q5 a) CD-ROMs are larger than floppy disks, so can store multimedia files normally found in CAL systems (1). CD ROMs cannot have the information stored on them overwritten, as they are 'read only'. This means no one can accidentally erase the information (1).

b) Sound can be used to tell the user how they are progressing on individual topics (1). Text can be used to tell a user whether they have answered a question correctly or not (1).

c) Any two answers from the following for 1 mark each:

- Hardware and software requirements for the system
- How to install the system
- How to use the system
- How to deal with errors

COMMENT For part (a), you will need to make these two points to get the marks. In part (b), you could talk about images and animation and how they could be used to give feedback. It is important to say how each type of media is used. In part (c), these are the main items you could put in your answer. Do not say 'user documentation'.

Q6 It reduces pressure to find places in prisons when they are full (1). It gives criminals more freedom, but keeps them to a set area because the tag would alert police if they went where they should not (1). Police will always know where the criminal is if the tag was set to tell them that (1). Equipment can be expensive for monitoring tags and for the tags themselves (1). Tags would have to be secure and waterproof to ensure they could not be taken off, otherwise they would be useless (1). Some might think that criminals should not be allowed to serve this type of sentence, as it is not severe enough (1).

COMMENT Each of the six points above could be included in your answer. You only need to choose any five points to gain full marks.

Q7 There are threats from hackers because they could gain access to confidential school information (1). Viruses could also be a problem, as staff and pupils may not be aware of the dangers of easily picking up viruses over the Internet (1). To protect the school, a firewall (1) could be installed to stop hackers, and user identification and passwords could be set up, especially on sensitive data (1). Backups could be used to ensure that the system could recover if there was a virus attack (1). A constantly updated anti-virus package should be installed to trap viruses (1). Staff and pupils should be trained about the threats (1).

COMMENT Each of the seven points above could be included in your answer. You only need to choose any five points to gain full marks.

INDEX

absolute cell references 37, 155
Access (software) 88, 89
accuracy 58, 64
actuators 8, 44
ADC (analogue-to-digital converters) 43
advertising 134, 135, 139, 140
   see also posters; web pages/sites
analogue-to-digital converters (ADC) 43
analysis 29, 30, 131-41
   client records problem 73-6
   price pledge task 111-13
   sports day programme 107-10
AND (logical operator) 39
animation 45
appliances, domestic 21, 46
applications 45-50
   in business 21, 48-9
   expert systems 50
   in the home 46-7
   multimedia systems 45
applications software 33, 35-42
   see also business applications software
arithmetic and logic units 9
arithmetic operators 37
ATMs (automatic teller machines) 21
AVERAGE (function) 37

backing storage 9, 13-14
   see also disks
backups 24, 31
   in project work 58, 65
banking 21, 27, 28, 38
   and encryption 24
bar codes 3, 4, 21
   and EPOS 48
   for library systems 49
batch headers 26
batch processing 26-7, 28
binary numbers 12, 34
book records 49
breakeven point 67-72
browsers 41
burglar alarms 21, 47
business applications 21, 48-9
business applications software 35-42
   Access 88, 89
   Excel 68, 72, 123
   Office XP 88, 89
   Publisher 62, 68, 88, 135
   Word 88, 115
bus topologies 17
buttons 92, 93, 94, 100
Button Wizard 92, 93
bytes 9

cables 15
CAD (computer-aided design) 3, 8, 22, 40
CAL (computer-aided learning) 45

cameras, digital 2
CD-ROMs 14
   see also Encarta
CD-Rs 14
CD-RWs 14
CDs (compact disks) 14
cells, spreadsheet 37
central-heating systems 21, 44, 47
central processing unit (CPU) 9
check-digit checks 27
chips
   on credit cards 5
   memory chips 9, 12
   as microprocessors 21, 46
columns, spreadsheet 37
commands 33
communication lines 41
communication networks 16
compact disks (CDs) 14
computer-aided design (CAD) 3, 8, 22, 40
computer-aided learning (CAL) 45
Computer Misuse Act (1990) 18
computers 9-11
   laptop computers 6, 7, 10
   linking together 15-17
concept keyboards 1
consistency 58, 63
control systems 28, 44
control totals 26
control units 9
copyright 18, 58, 65
CPU (central processing unit) 9
credit cards 5, 21
criteria *see* performance criteria
cropping images 58, 61

data 24-5, 31
   binary storage of 12
   links between 139
   modelling *see* modelling
   processing 26-8
      in project work 131
      databases 147-9
      posters 137, 138
      on spreadsheets 37
   validity *see* validation
   see also databases; information
databases 38-9
   client records 75, 76, 77-105
   stock control 136, 139, 140
      design 147-52
      evaluation 174
      implementation 161-5
      testing 168-72
data-capture forms 148, 161-2
   see also data-entry
data controller 19

data entry 38, 92
   design 81-4, 148-9
   testing 100, 168, 170, 172
data logging 43
Data Protection Acts (1984 and 1998) 19, 65
Data Protection Commissioner (DPC) 19
data structures 31, 38
   designing 77-80
   implementing 90-4
data subjects 19, 20
data types 31, 38
   in project work 77, 78, 79, 148
design 29, 31
   databases 77-87, 147-52
      interfaces 81-4
      outputs 85-7
   publishing 114-16, 142-6
   spreadsheets 121-4, 153-6
   see also CAD
design specifications 29, 31
Design view 93, 97
desktop microcomputers 10, 50
desktop publishers *see* DTP
development, system 29, 31
digital cameras 2
digital signals 2, 41
digital telephones 47
digital versatile disks (DVDs) 14
direct changeover 29, 32
disks 10, 13, 14, 33
   formatting 13, 34
documents 30, 35-6
   posters *see* posters
   programmes 58-66, 107-10, 114-20
   questionnaires *see* questionnaires
   user documentation 31, 101-3, 115-17
   see also publishing
domestic appliances 21, 46
dot-matrix printers 6
download information 41
drop-down menus 161-2, 174
DTP (desktop publishers) 35-6, 58-66, 144
   see also Publisher
DVDs (digital versatile disks) 14

editing designs 40
editing text 35, 36, 62
Electronic Point-Of-Sale terminals (EPOS) 48
e-mail 16, 22, 41-2
   in publishing sub-problem 134, 136
Encarta 58, 59, 60
encoding data 24
encryption 24
EPOS (Electronic Point-Of-Sale terminals) 48

errors 58, 62, 66
  and user documentation 101, 103
  and user testing 98, 100
evaluation 173-4
  client record database 104-5
  modelling problem 67, 72
    price pledge 129
  sports-day programme 119-20
Excel 68, 72, 123
expert systems 50

feasibility studies 29
feedback 44, 45
fibre-optic cables 15
fields 31, 38
  client-record problem 77-80, 90, 91
  stock-control problem 147-8, 152, 174
files 2, 34
file servers 16
financial models 67
  see also profit calculations
floppy disks 13
flow diagrams 30
foreign key fields 38
formatting cells 37
formatting disks 13, 34
formatting text 35, 36
forms 38, 92, 100, 148-9, 161-2
  see also data-entry
formulae 37, 68
  business-profits problem 154, 155, 166-7, 172
  price-pledge problem 122, 123, 125, 127-8
Form Wizard 92, 93, 97
frames 35, 36, 62
fraud 18, 21
functions 37, 67, 69, 70

gigahertz 10
graphics manipulation 115
  see also images
graphics packages 144
graphics tablets 3
graphs 58, 60
GUI (graphical user interface) 33

hacking 16, 18, 21
hard copy *see* printouts; screen dumps
hard disks 10, 13, 33
hardware 9-11
  identifying requirements 73, 76, 88-9
  specification 31
  see also input devices; output devices
hash totals 26
headed paper 142, 145, 158-9, 174
headphones 7
health issues 23, 58, 65
hit rates 26, 27
home applications 46, 47
home workers 22

hyperlinks 41, 160
IF (function) 37
images 58, 59, 60, 63
  cropping 58, 61
  and multimedia systems 45
  see also graphics
implementation 29, 32
  data structures 90-4
  price-pledge problem 125-6
  shop problem 157-67
  sports-day programme 117-18
inference engine 50
information 131, 132, 137, 138
  database problems 73, 74, 105, 147
  publishing problems 58, 59, 142
    sports-day programme 108-9
  spreadsheet problems 112, 153
  see also data
initial investigations 29
inkjet printers 6
input devices 1-5, 9
input forms *see* forms
inputs 31, 44
  client-record database 73, 90-4, 103
  home applications 46, 47
  sports-day programme 109
interface design 81-4
  see also data-entry
internal memory 9, 12
  RAM 9, 10, 12, 33
Internet 19, 21, 28, 41
  and encryption 24
  in project work 58, 59, 61, 65
  for teleworking 22
  and viruses 25
Internet Service Providers (ISPs) 28, 41, 42
interviews 29, 30
  for projects 73, 74, 132
ISDN lines 41
ISPs (Internet Service Providers) 28, 41, 42

jobs 22
joysticks 1

keyboards 1, 10
key fields 26, 31, 38
  in project work 147, 161
knowledgebases 50

LANs (local area networks) 16
laptop computers 6, 7, 10
laser printers 7
layering 58, 60, 63
layouts 58, 60, 63
LCD (liquid crystal display) monitors 6
legal issues 18-20
letter-headed paper 142, 145, 158-9, 174
libraries 4, 40, 49
licences 18

loan records 49
local area networks (LANs) 16
logical operators 37, 39
logos 139, 142, 145, 157, 159
look-up tables 91

machine code 34
magnetic disks 13
magnetic ink character readers (MICRs) 5
magnetic strip readers 5
magnetic tape 13
magnetised ink 5
mail-merge letters 85, 88-9, 95-7, 100, 165
  evaluation 104, 174
  in user guides 176
mainframe computers 11
masks (databases) 91
master files 26, 27, 28
master forms *see* templates
mathematical operators 67, 68, 69
MAX (function) 37
megahertz 10
member records 49
memory 9, 12
  RAM 9, 10, 12, 33
microcomputers 10, 50
microphones 2
microprocessors 21, 46
  see also chips
MICRs (magnetic ink character readers) 5
midi instruments 2
MIN (function) 37
minicomputers 10
misuse 18
Model Builder 68
modelling 37, 67-72
  pricing problem 111-13, 121-9
modems 41
monitoring systems 29
monitors 6, 10
motors 8, 44
mouse 1, 10
multimedia systems 45
music, midi instruments for 2

network cards 15
networks 15, 16-17
notebook computers 10

observation 29, 30, 73, 74
OCRs (optical character readers) 5
Office XP (software) 88, 89
OMRs (optical mark readers) 4
online processing 28
operating systems 12, 33
optical character readers (OCRs) 5
optical disks 14
optical mark readers (OMRs) 4
OR (logical operator) 39

outcomes 109-10, 113, 131, 137-8
  evaluating 119, 120, 129, 173, 174
  specifying 140-1
output devices 6-8, 9
outputs 31, 32, 44
  home applications 46, 47
  project work 131, 137, 138
    databases 73, 85-7, 90-4, 149-50
    price modelling 112
    sports-day programme 108-9

parallel running 29, 32
passive infra-red sensors (PIRs) 43, 47
passwords 16, 24, 31
payroll 27, 48
performance criteria 131, 140-1
  database problem 174
  modelling task 113, 129
  publishing problem 146, 173
  sports-day programme 109-10, 119-20
phased changeover 29, 32
physical protection 24
pictures 35
pilot running 29, 32
piracy 18
PIRs (passive infra-red sensors) 43, 47
pixels 6
plans, project 143-4
  databases 147-9
  spreadsheets 153-5
  see also test plans
plotters 8
point and click 33
postcodes 91, 102
posters
  shop problem 134, 135, 137-8, 140
    design 142, 143, 144
    evaluation 173
    implementation 157-8
  sports day 58-66
predictions in projects 67, 71
presence checks 27
presentations 45
printers 6-7, 88-9
printouts
  publishing problem 62, 117-18
  spreadsheet problem 125-6
  see also screen dumps/shots
processing 26-8, 46, 73
processors see microprocessors
process tests 169, 171
product codes 4
profit calculations
  breakeven point 67-72
  shop problem 133, 134, 135, 136, 139
    implementation 166-7
    information required 153
    outcomes 141
    user guides 177
programme of events 58-66, 107-10, 114-20

programming languages 34
project identification 29
Publisher (software) 62, 68, 88, 135
publishing
  DTP 35-6, 58-66, 144
  mail-merges see mail-merge
  shop problem 134, 135-6, 140
    design 142-6
    evaluation 173
    implementation 157-60
  word-processing see word processing
  see also documents

queries 38, 39, 93, 95, 96-7
  evaluation 105
  testing 99
  in user documentation 102, 176
questionnaires 29, 30, 73, 74, 132
  for user testing 100, 105
queuing models 67

radio wave transmission 15
RAM (random-access memory) 9, 10, 12, 33
range checks 27
read-only memory (ROM) 9, 12
real-time 28, 44
records 38, 148
  in user documentation 101-3
relational databases 140
relationships 38, 150-1, 163
  between sub-problems 139, 145, 156
Repetitive Strain Injury (RSI) 23
replication 37, 166-7
reports 38, 100, 150, 152
  design 85-7, 97
  evaluation 105
  in user documentation 102, 103
Report Wizard 93
requirements specifications 29, 30
  see also user requirements
research, beginning 131-2
resolution, screen 6
reusable solutions 131, 132
  database 175-6
  publishing 134, 137, 138, 140, 142
    evaluation 173
    implementation 158
    justifying software 144
  spreadsheets 153, 166, 177
  websites 143, 144, 160
ring topologies 17
ROM (read-only memory) 9, 12
rows, spreadsheet 37
RSI (Repetitive Strain Injury) 23

safety issues 23, 65
satellites 15
saving work 24-5, 58, 64, 65
scanners 3, 4
scenarios 73, 75
screen dumps/shots 31

databases 92-3, 97
  modelling problems 112
  publishing problems 58, 59, 64, 66, 157-60
  in user documentation 101-2
  see also printouts
screens (monitors) 6, 10
  see also data-entry
search engines 41
searches
  databases 147, 149, 152
    evaluation 174
    implementation 162, 164
    testing 169, 171
    user guide 176
  Internet 58, 59
security 16
sensors 3, 28, 43, 47
  for control systems 44
servers 16
social issues 21-2
software
  applications software 33, 35-42
  business applications 35-42
    Access 88, 89
    Excel 68, 72, 123
    Office XP 88, 89
    Publisher 62, 68, 88, 135
    Word 88, 115
  combining 95-7
  comparing with non-ICT solutions 135-6
  databases 88, 89, 90, 152
  identifying requirements 73, 76, 88-9
  justifying choices 115-16, 144-5, 152, 155-6
  licences and copyright 18
  for modelling 67, 68, 123
  for networking 15
  for OCRs 5
  specifying 31
  systems software 33-4
  virus-checking software 25
sorting
  databases 38, 149, 152, 163
    testing 169, 171
  spreadsheets 37
sound 2, 7, 45
speakers 7
speed, processor 10, 11
spell-checking 58, 64, 96, 144
spider diagrams 132, 139
spreadsheets 10, 37
  design 153-6
  for graphs 61
  implementation 166-7
  for modelling 68-72, 121-8
  and relationships 139
  testing 172
standalone computers 15

star topologies 17
stock-control 21, 48
  in project work 133, 134, 136, 139, 140
    design 144, 150, 151
    evaluation 174
    implementation 161-5
    testing 168-71
    user guides 175-7
storage 12-14, 33, 34
  see also backing storage; internal memory
sub-problems 130-41
  database 147-52, 161-5, 168-72, 174
  links between 131, 132, 139
    database sub-problem 151
    publishing sub-problem 145
  publishing 134, 135-6, 157-60, 173
    designing for 142-6
  spreadsheets 153-6, 166-7, 172
SUM (function) 37
supercomputers 11
supermarkets 4, 16, 21, 48
switches 8
systems 29-32
  central-heating systems 21, 44, 47
  control systems 44
  expert systems 50
  library systems 49
  multimedia systems 45
  operating systems 33
  real-time systems 44
  stock-control systems 21
systems software 33-4

tables 35, 38
  design 147, 148, 150-1
  evaluation 174
  implementation 163
  linking 104, 105, 150-1, 163, 164
  testing with 168-9, 171

telephones 22, 41, 47
teleworking 22
templates 144
  posters 134, 140, 142, 144
    evaluation 173
    implementation 158
  spreadsheets 156, 166-7
  website 159, 160
testing 29, 31, 32
  databases 168-71
    client records 98-100
  predictions 67, 71
  publishing problems 146
    sports-day programme 110, 116
  spreadsheets 124, 127-8, 156, 172
    price 113, 124, 127-8
test plans 31, 32
  databases 168-9
  publishing problems 146
  spreadsheets 124, 127-8, 156
text boxes 157, 173
topologies, network 17
tracker balls 1
training 29, 32
transcribing data 26
translators 33, 34

user documentation 31, 101-3, 175-7
user-IDs 16, 24
user input 46, 47
user interface 31, 33, 50
user requirements 29, 30, 73, 75
  evaluation 104
  see also requirements specification
user testing 32, 98-100
utilities 33, 34

validation 26, 27, 31, 38
  in project work 148, 152, 161
    evaluation 174
    testing 99, 168, 170, 172
VDUs (visual display units) 6, 10
verification of data 26, 27
video-conferencing 22
video digitisers 2
video recorders 47
viruses 16, 18, 25, 34
  in project work 58, 66
visual display units (VDUs) 6, 10

WANs (wide area networks) 16
web pages/sites 41
  shop problem 134, 136, 140
    design 143, 144, 145
    implementation 159-60
  see also World Wide Web (WWW)
wide area networks (WANs) 16
WIMP environments 33
wire cables 15
wireless data transmission 15
Wizards 72, 92, 93, 97
word processing 10, 33, 35, 36
  for client records 75, 76, 88-9, 95-7, 104
  and DTP 66
  in research 132
  see also publishing
Word (software) 88, 115
World Wide Web (WWW) 41
  see also web pages/sites